CARING WOMEN:

The Good Daughter Syndrome

Parent Care with Less Guilt

By Elana Peters,
MA, CMC (ret.)

Book design and computer production
by Patty Arnold, *Menagerie Design & Publishing*

The stories contained in this book were collected over the past 40 years. Although they are real, the names were changed to protect privacy.

Other Books by Elana Peters

Hard Questions, Simple Answers:
A Workbook to Take the Crisis out of Caregiving

A Preguntas Difíciles, Respuestas Fáciles,
Spanish Translation

Website

https://caring-women.com

Printed in the United States of America
ISBN # 1-893775-04-6

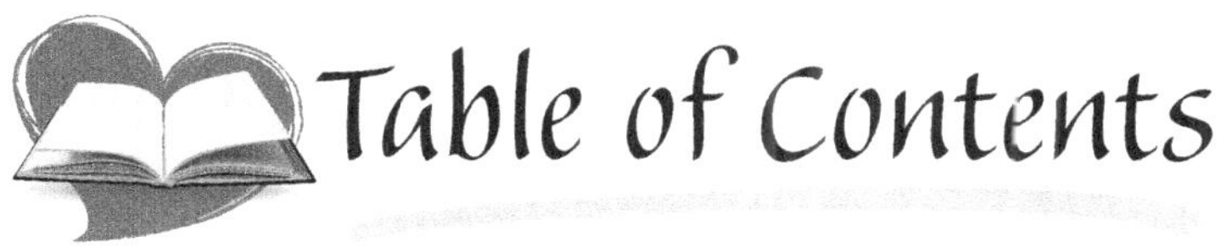

Table of Contents

Introduction: Your Parents Are Who They Are. 4

Chapter 1 Expectations and Reality 7

Chapter 2 Caregiving: An Emotional Seesaw 20

Chapter 3 Sibling Rivalry: Really? 32

Chapter 4 Setting Boundaries in Caregiving 41

Chapter 5 Communication: Finding Common Ground . . . 51

Chapter 6 Avoiding Caregiver Burnout. 62

Chapter 7 Dementia: Symptoms and Treatments 73

Chapter 8 Driving: When is it Time to Stop? 90

Chapter 9 Mortality: The End of a Journey 101

Chapter 10 Men as Caregivers: It's Just Different 119

Chapter 11 Decision Making 101:
Making the Difficult Choice 130

Staying at Home 133

Moving In With An Adult Child 137

Moving to Alternative Living Environment 146

Chapter 12 Everyday Heroes and the Rewards 159

Resources to Help

Glossary: Health and Social Services Terms 165

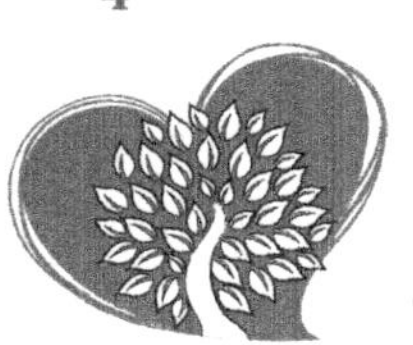

Introduction:

Your Parents Are Who They Are

Meeting your parents as aging adults is often like seeing your classmates at the high school reunion. The faces look familiar and you know you should remember what they were like. After spending a short time with them, you remember a lot, the good and the bad.

I remember the day this analogy came home to me. My mother called from her hospital bed late on a Friday evening, describing in mournful detail her current health crisis. She said the pain was intense, the infection wouldn't respond to the drugs, and *this* time she was going to die. Since the hospital was 60 miles away, I told her I'd be there early the next morning. I hastily rearranged my plans and had my three teenaged daughters do the same. All of us felt a little selfish for being inconvenienced and yet we knew it was our duty to show love and support, as this might be the last time we saw Nana.

Bright and early on Saturday, we took off for the arduous drive to the hospital. Two blocks from my home, my fuel line broke and I had to borrow my neighbor's chugging car. Almost two hours later, fighting freeway traffic all the way, we arrived to be welcomed by my mother standing in the doorway of her hospital room wearing a black negligee, claiming, "A miracle has taken place. Isn't that wonderful?"

Then she took a scornful look at the four of us and asked why we were dressed in jeans. "I've talked so much about you to the nursing staff, and I wanted to be proud of you." It was same mother, same manipulation, same criticisms, just a different day.

Perhaps, like my former classmates, I thought age might mellow those annoying traits that I remembered when I was younger. After hearing my mother's sighing and sorrowful description, I imagined our arrival to be met with appreciation. How hurt and disappointed I was. My daughters were totally surprised and became angry with me for making them change their plans. They were expecting to find their Nana near death. So here I was, sandwiched between two generations, not satisfying either one. I then realized that I was expecting a different mother, one who had changed.

I thought I had been a good daughter in coming as quickly as I could. Somehow that was not enough. Too often, we caring adult daughters try to make our parents, who really are the same people they were when we were younger, be happy, content and satisfied with their present lives, which is quite an impossible task. They are aging and in decline and may have limitations in their daily lives. They don't like it and we become the scapegoats for their frustrations. This is when we find ourselves discouraged and exhausted in trying to make their lives better. This is the experience of **The Good Daughter Syndrome**.

Caring Women are everywhere. You are one of them. You care what happens to your family, your job, your coworkers and yet, when faced with the care of an older adult, you can be overwhelmed by the tasks involved.

This book is about finding the balance between caring for your parent and caring for yourself as well as the other loved ones in your life. You will find helpful **Caring Woman Tips** at the end of each chapter to make the challenges of caregiving easier to accomplish, while reducing the guilt and protecting yourself from caregiver *burnout*.[1]

[1] **Caregivers pay the ultimate price for providing care – increased mortality**. Elderly caregivers (aged 66-96) who experience caregiving-related stress have a **63% higher mortality rate than non caregivers of the same age**.

Family Caregiver Alliance of the National Center on Aging, 2006

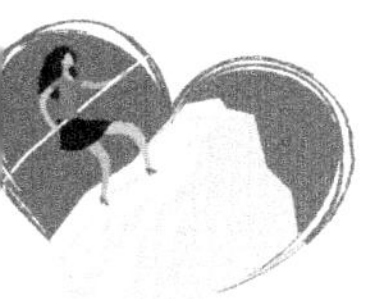

Chapter 1:

Expectations and Reality

Most of you did not really think you would have to care for your parents. Sometimes a little denial helps us cope and yet caring for aging parents is a frequent reality today. More than likely, this will be one of the most emotional yet valuable experiences in your lifetime.

The Good Daughter is the woman who is trying-to-do-it-all-and-be-a-total-success-at-everything-to-everyone-in-her-life, often forgetting about herself, which means putting herself last. You may have a spouse, children, a career, and other responsibilities to your home and community. However, no matter how busy you are or how far you rise in your career or in your community, at the end of the day, you bear the emotional responsibility of your family.

How did women get this way? It is in their genetic code, so when they had babies they would be fed, nurtured and cared for. It is historical in that it has always been this way. Women are socialized to be the caregivers. However, male siblings usually get "the knight in shining armor" award from their parents even though the daughter is the one taking on more of the caring responsibilities. And last but not least, it is cultural. When your spouse or your friends ask why you put up with all of this and keep on doing it, you answer, "I am the daughter. I am *supposed* to do this."

Too often, the caring woman is resistant to asking for or getting help. You don't ask because you are good daughters and want to make everything "right." Many times you go to extremes in your attempts to make others happy, to feel better, or to stop complaining—and sometimes it is because you want to win your parents' approval.

Why are you trying to do all and everything by yourself? Do you think it is your duty? Do you think you are the only one who can give the "right kind" of care? Are you afraid that your older adult will criticize or make your life miserable if you seek outside help?

If you think you can do it all and not have it effect you, you will be in serious trouble, physically, mentally and/or emotionally. There are countless studies that show caregivers are more prone to high blood pressure, depression and illness than the older adult who is receiving the care. And the loving daughter caregiver has a 44% chance of becoming seriously ill or dying before the older adult receiving the care.

Yes, it's true! If you keep trying to-do-it-all without reprieve, respite, or supplemental help from family, friends or paid care providers, you will get sick and/or depressed. What happens is that the constant and ongoing care and stress will compromise your immune system and it becomes depleted. Trying to do it all will affect your health, quickly turning you into the second patient. Then who is going to give the care to the older adult?

You may have come into this role as the result of a healthcare crisis, a gradual decline or even observing some subtle indicators, such as Mom being neglectful of her hygiene, or learning that Dad has fallen several times or finding moldy food in the refrigerator. These can be the early signs of more serious issues facing you in the very near future. There is no quick fix when your parent starts to decline in mind or body. It will be up to you, the caring woman, **The Good Daughter**, to help your parent. You will have the responsibility of assessing the situation, finding the appropriate resources and then following through with your parent. This last one is where caregiving gets complicated.

In the following pages you will find specific strategies to help you find your way. There are brief stories that tell how some family caregivers problem-solved or faced the challenges brought about by their own doubts, and criticisms from family and friends. These practical suggestions come from my 40 years of working with caregiving families of older adults as a hospital discharge planner, then in social services at a senior center, a home care agency, a retirement facility and, finally, as a geriatric care manager.

You will need to know and accept that caregiving an older adult is not easy and involves many varied and progressive tasks. It can also call into question your caregiving skills as your parent's health and/or mental capabilities can change from hour to hour, day to day, or stay static for weeks or months. You never know what the day will bring, especially if the parent has dementia. Caregiving can be emotional as you face the loss of a loving parent, or frustrating as you realize that you may never have the parent's cooperation or gratitude.

Caring Women and Responsibility [2]

In years past, the conflicts involved with caring for older relatives were not discussed. Everyone just coped because families knew it would not be for very long. More often than not when older people got sick, they usually died within six months to a year. A caring woman could endure discomfort for short periods of time because she knew it would end soon. Advances in medical technology have irreversibly changed the way older adults live and the way they die. You now face obstacles that were never faced by women in previous generations. In turn, you must now change the way you think about older adults and the way you care for them.

Many caring women were raised to believe that taking care of a frail and aging parent is their sole responsibility. If you take on the whole burden without help, you will wear out and will be no good to anyone. You will need to find some balance by asking for help from others, seeking out appropriate resources, and finding some "down time" where you can reenergize. This involves setting boundaries, which is not always an easy task, but a necessity if you are to survive. Yes, *survival*, as many women may become ill or die before the aging parent.

---

2 Three quarters of caregivers are women.
National Institute on Aging, 2015

Susan's Story: *Susan, recently retired from a successful career as buyer for a major upscale retailer, was having great difficulty managing her mother's care. Dorothy, her mother, a former social worker, seemed to know all the tricks to manipulate and frustrate her daughter, including verbal criticism. The son, David, lived on the East Coast, called once a week, and of course was seen as Mr. Wonderful. Dorothy understood that "David was way too busy to visit. However, it was so nice for him to call. He really cares."*

Dorothy needed 24-hour supervised care, as she was having problems with balance. As the months passed, she fell three or four times, badly bruising herself, but refused to go to a doctor. In addition, she was often forgetting to turn off the water, both inside and outside the house. The neighbors reported her to Adult Protective Services several times. However, when the social workers came to evaluate her, she managed to get up to speed and fool them.

This scenario went on for almost three years. Meanwhile, Susan was having symptoms of stress both physically and emotionally. What was she to do? Well, Dorothy fell and broke a hip, which required hospitalization and rehabilitation. Susan made the wise decision to move her mother directly from rehab to a Residential Care Facility, where she would be safe and well-cared for as she gradually declined into advanced stages of dementia.

Throughout this time, Susan had stomach symptoms that she ignored, since trying to "fix" her mother's situation took priority over herself. When Susan finally did go to the doctor, she was diagnosed with pancreatic cancer. Her stress overload produced inflammation, which many times can lead to cancer. Eighteen months later Susan died. The stress of caregiving can be deadly.

What a sad ending for this lovely woman who cared so much and yet was curtailed by a manipulative mother. Dorothy held Susan responsible for her own memory loss and personal unhappiness. Throughout her life, Dorothy held up David, and then Susan's husband, Sam, as examples of goodness and maleness. Unsaid was the fact that she held the male species to be better human beings. David had moved across the country to get away from his mother's neediness and now he was the hero. Even though she tried and tried, Susan could never measure up to David and Sam. Not fair, you say? No, it's not. However, that situation takes place all too frequently in caregiving families.

You may be attempting to be the perfect caregiver and the perfect daughter. That is unachievable. The unspoken expectation in our society is that women are to be the family caregiver to all in their family and especially to the older parents or parents-in-law when they begin their decline into old age and death. Trying to be all things to everyone in your life is unrealistic. You can burnout, become depressed, critically ill, or die. [3]

---

[3] Mental, emotional & physical health can be negatively affected., *AARP & National Partnership Study for Women & Families*, 2018

Why are you caregiving?

Has the need for caregiving your parent come upon you suddenly? Maybe you have noticed recently a decline in their behavior or a change in their personality. Sometimes with dementia the changes are subtle and the aging parent can fool family and friends for months or even longer. However, these subtleties can change overnight and you will need to be ready to address this challenge as it is only just the beginning of the caregiving journey.

A question for you: What is the reason you are caregiving? It is important to evaluate your reason for caregiving as it will strongly affect the outcome of this experience. Is this a gift you are repaying for your parent's care, or is it due to a feeling of obligation and/or duty? Depending on your motives, you will either have acceptance and a sense of peace, or have an experience that is full of negativity and resentment. If you have had a good relationship with your parent, then your caregiving time will enable you to cope with the often frustrating and heartrending experience of watching a loved one diminish and die.

The caring daughter who becomes a caregiver out of duty or by default will have a more difficult time coping with the negative emotions that come as a natural part of caregiving. If you feel as though you "have to do it" or "should do it," feelings of frustration, resentment and anger will rise to the surface over and over again. These feelings are usually followed by guilt because you had these feelings in the first place.

You may ask yourself why you have to be the caregiver. This is especially true if you did not have a good relationship with your parent in your early years. The duty-filled caregiver suffers even more if abuse or abandonment was a part of the past. Although issues from the past may have been hidden or buried for many years, they will be remembered and become part of the present caregiving experience.

If caregiving is seen as a debt to be repaid, you will be in a no-win situation. The older parent may have brought you into this world and raised you, however there is no way you can repay them for that. Raising a child and caring for an older parent are two very different situations. When one raises a child, there are ages and stages of growth and development; there are goals and expectations as the child grows more and more independent. A parent watches a child open up to a future, where an adult daughter watches her parent close down the past.

Every parent needs help at one time or another. The difficulty is that there is no way to predict at what age a critical change in health may occur. Aging loved ones are individuals and are vastly different from one another. The differences in the aging process vary widely and from individual to individual according to their personality, their ethnicity, their nationality, their life experiences and their previous coping skills. For better or for worse, dear daughters, you have inherited your parents, and must cope with them to the best of your ability, without sacrificing your physical and emotional health.

To Be or Not To Be the Hands-On Caregiver

Caregiving presents as *a continuum of care with changes* and the need to adapt to these changes will present many challenges. Throughout this book you will find examples and stories of ways to cope and set limits with these challenges.

> ***Ms. B's Story:*** *One of my first clients as a Geriatric Care manager (GCM) was Ms. B, an adult daughter and only child, who lived out of state and was estranged from her father. She requested care management services to assess her father's health status and to find him an appropriate alternative living situation. She said her father, Tom F, was in declining physical health with early dementia and was calling her constantly to yell at her for not being there to help him.*
>
> *At the time I was surprised by Ms. B's extremely matter-of-fact, business-like voice and manner. After several phone conversations, Ms. B finally told me that her father had been an abusive alcoholic when she was growing up. She stated that she was willing and able to pay for her father's care however, she added that she could not possibly visit or be personally involved with him due to the horrendous physical and emotional pain she suffered in the past.*

Pleased that the Ms. B shared this with me, I told her I understood and thought her wise that she honored her father by finding the care Tom F needed without thinking she needed to be a physically present caregiver.

If keeping her distance would keep her mentally and emotionally safe, then that is how Ms. B was protecting herself from resurrecting the past and enduring more pain. Too often adult children from an abusive childhood have hopeful expectations that the parent will apologize for the past and show appreciation. Chances are this will not happen and you will be reduced to the child you were then, thinking that their behavior is your fault.

Having a parent who has neglected or abused you, and then wanting you to be the caring daughter is not realistic. Quite often an older parent wants nurturing when they themselves were not nurturing. If they apologize for the past, it may make the situation easier and, yet, the past is not forgotten, especially if the abuse continues through name calling and criticism. It is truly disheartening that more adult children do not come to terms with an abusive past rather than attempting by overcompensation, wanting the parent to acknowledge the past and apologize. An adult child cannot change the aging, declining parent any more than they can change the past.

Being the Primary Caregiver is Not an Easy Task

Whether by choice or default, the caregiving role will not be, for numerous reasons, an easy task. Caregiving is a demanding, time consuming, energy-robbing experience that requires action, patience, planning and flexibility. The difficult demands and continuous changes may be somewhat offset by the personal benefits received. However, you as a caregiver may reach a time when the demands outweigh the benefits, especially if you find yourself physically or emotionally exhausted. These stresses can negatively affect your health, attitude, relationships, career and more. It can affect your ability to be the kind of caregiver you want to be, which only adds to the exhaustion and stress.

Becoming a primary caregiver makes you the person upon whom the older adult can depend. This means watching a once active and capable adult declines into childlike behaviors and diminished abilities. This alone can be heartbreaking. Add to it an older adult's lack of cooperation and seeming ingratitude, then frustration and anger will become your constant companions. If the caregiving situation becomes overwhelming, then this is the time to look into an alternative living arrangement. As the primary caregiver, you are the one who will try to locate, discern the quality, appropriateness, and affordability of the resources that fit your parent's needs.

Then about the time you have completed these efforts, your parent may become resistant and insist on not spending the money. They may tell you that they are perfectly capable of staying at home, however, they are not. The parent is only still at home because you are helping. If you are near exhaustion and frustrated, then changes will have to be made and the rainy-day money spent on their care. This is the time when you become instrumental in helping the older adult make care choices.

As a caring daughter, you have assumed the responsibility for the older adult's well-being. Although you may feel as though you are in charge of your parent's life, you are not. This older parent, unless severely mentally impaired, needs to maintain as much choice in their care as possible and as much independence as their health will allow. Meanwhile you may have to sit on the sidelines waiting for them to make the choices that are in their best interests. Underlying this resistance is the parent's strong desire to remain in control and not have anyone other than you assist them.

As a caring woman you want to feel that the older parent is safe, reasonably comfortable, and is as content as possible under the circumstances. After much effort in locating appropriate resources, the older parent may manipulate you into thinking that you do have their cooperation, then an hour or a day later accuse you of treating them like a child or trying to put them away so you can take their money. They do not perceive your attempts at helping them as loving or caring. Is it any wonder you are in turmoil?

Chapter #1 - CARING WOMAN TIPS

1. **Whatever needs to be done must be done *with* the parent not *for* the parent.** The key to successful caregiving is allowing the older parent as much control over their life as possible. Even parents who are suffering from dementia can have wishes and opinions, even though they may not be realistic. Take the time to listen to their stories and their needs, hearing their underlying fears. Ask gentle questions about their feelings in certain situations, and why they might feel that way. *You listen so they feel important and that their opinion matters.*

2. **Although each family's caregiving situation is unique, approaching the caregiving situation cautiously can make it run more smoothly.** If you move forward with too much too soon, the older parent will feel as if they are losing control. Taking over their lives and telling them what should be done is not going to work. *Of course the exception to this is a health crisis, when the parent needs emergency help or immediate placement.*

3. **If you see signs of decline in your parent either physically or mentally, then begin immediately to look into what is available in your community.** Caregiving has so many aspects. All of them need to be managed in the light of the older parent's physical, intellectual and emotional capabilities...and their finances. Attempting to think all of them through at one time and come to any immediate decisions can overwhelm you.

4. **Progress slowly but surely; then you can accomplish your goal of understanding what is best for your parent with their input.**

Chapter 2:

Caregiving: An Emotional Seesaw

You're a caring woman, a good daughter and a responsible person.

Caregiving to an older adult family member is different than any previous experience you may have had. The journey of caregiving will challenge your talents, your time and, most of all, your emotions.

The variety of emotions can run the gamut from loving tenderness to unbridled fury. Having negative emotions can make you feel guilty even though all of your emotions and feelings are real and normal. Most caregivers have these feelings and they may go on for days, weeks or months. Resentment may build because no one seems to understand the difficulties you're dealing with or offers to help you. As time passes you may begin to feel hopeless, which makes you feel even worse, adding feelings of guilt for having negative feelings in the first place. It's an exhausting and vicious cycle.

What can you do to lessen the emotional cost of providing care? Accept from the beginning that you cannot be all things to your older parent. It is also very important to realize that you cannot make them well or happy.

The Resnick's Story: *The Resnicks, Barry and Ruth, longtime friends of mine are extremely wealthy and were visiting from out of state. Over the years Barry had shared the challenges of his aging mother with me. Besides Barry, the senior Mrs. Resnick had two other sons and various relatives living close by who visited, took her shopping and out to lunch or dinner. Their efforts to get her interested in something besides her aging and health complaints were futile.*

During dinner one evening, Barry asked me if I would come and care for his mother. He said he would pay me a million dollars, and he was just half serious. I asked him if his mother was ever a happy person. He replied "Of course not!" I told him I sympathized with his situation, however, I did not need a million dollars that badly!

As your parents age, they do not see themselves as aging because their spirit feels the same. Their personality remains the same, unless they are in the advanced stages of dementia. If your older parent was not happy, content, or easy to be with earlier in life, do not expect them to start now. If you are still trying to win their approval and praise, you will probably be disappointed.

Through the trials and errors of life, you have probably learned that love is not always nice, sweet or, at times, easy. Love is an action word, not just a feeling. As an action, love involves considerable patience, endurance and forgiveness. When caring women become caregivers, they need to be realistic in their assessment of the present situation. Your older parent is still the same person they always were only now they are losing their strength and energy. In the struggle to maintain independence and control, the parent uses up much of the energy reserved for being courteous and grateful. So you will need to find the appreciation you deserve in other ways: from family, friends or a support group.

Meanwhile give yourself a pat on the back and a big hug. *You are doing an incredible job* and by reading this book and using the tips at the end of each chapter, you will find it easier to cope.

Are You Parenting Your Parent?

No, it just feels like it. Many articles and several books have been written about the time in life when you become your parent's parent. It may feel like it but you will never become your parent's parent. Your parent has been an active, independent adult. Although they may dig in their heels at times and behave in childlike ways, it does not mean that they need you to make their decisions. You do, however, change roles. As you observe your parent becoming frail and increasingly dependent, your role in their life will change. As your role changes, you will gently and kindly help them make the decisions for their well-being and safety.

These changes are the natural evolution of the seasons in life. Watching the many changes taking place in your parent's life, you may question their ability to live independently. As you start the caregiving process and need to assume more and more responsibility, your older parent will grow increasingly dependent. This increasing dependency is what makes you feel as though you are the parent. This is called role reversal. It is the feeling of role reversal that brings with it frustration and conflict.

Experiencing confusion about your role is natural. You may not know the best time to step in or step back and let your parent find out the hard way the consequences of making inappropriate decisions for their care and safety. If the parent is suffering from dementia, most likely they are "unlearning." Reminding them again and again to do particular tasks, such as the schedule of taking meds, *will not work*. Their short term memory is disappearing.

Becoming responsible for your parent's care may bring up sensitive feelings and unresolved issues from the past. These issues could very much become a part of the current situation. Such as:

- **A narcissistic parent whose whole world is about them.** They do not want your advice or input and often defy doctor's orders or those of the DMV.
- **Sibling rivalry that can interfere with the decisions being made.** Your out-of-town brother just visited and thought Mom was fine, as she often rises to "the occasion."
- **Your mother's lifelong adversity about going to the doctor.** "I'm healthy and doing just fine," she declares, even though you visit daily to make sure Mom remembered to eat the dinner you left in the refrigerator and has taken her meds.

- **Your mother tells you how she took care of her aunt and later on her mother.** Times were different sixty or seventy years ago. People only lived on the average about six months to a year after they became seriously ill. [4]

The above challenges can be difficult to manage in light of all the other issues you may face. These issues can be sensitive and, if not handled properly, can add to your turmoil. *It is your mission to rise above past issues and focus on the necessary practical ones that need to be resolved in the present.* Attending a support group can help you to resolve issues since many of these caregivers have faced the same challenges and can offer constructive ways to handle them.

Guilt: The Gift that Keeps on Giving

The above statement by Erma Bombeck may strike a familiar chord in your heart and in the hearts of the millions women in this country who are caring for their frail and aging relatives. These caring women are attempting by their heroic caregiving efforts to keep their loved ones out of institutions. Ninety percent of frail older adults live in their own homes or with relatives.

These caring family members provide for all their needs and yet they feel guilty because they think they have not done enough. "I feel so guilty" is the frequent refrain of caring

---

[4] **Fact:** Medical technology has advanced life expectancy, but not always its quality. So more people are living longer with one or more limitations with which they need help.

women. Is this true guilt or just the feelings associated with the inability to make Mother happy or find the right doctor or treatment that can make Dad feel better?

True guilt is the result of an individual deliberately hurting another or committing an action that breaks the law. Caring for an older parent is certainly not a wrong action. Caregiving at its highest level is done out of love for another. Even if caregiving is done out of a sense of duty or obligation, it is still honoring one's parent.

Caring for your older parents means they are not to be ignored, shunned or neglected. Older parents are to be assisted and honored. The challenge is in knowing how to fulfill your loving obligation to them within their physical and mental limitations, yet also within the framework of your personal responsibilities, in a way that will create the least amount of guilt.

Your acceptance of your parent's present situation will go a long way in helping to lessen your guilt. Accept the fact that your parent is not going to change. They have been who they are for a long time. If anything, illness and failing health exacerbate the negative personality traits and overrule many social skills. *Accept that your parent is not going to get better.* Sometimes they may seem to improve for a while, which lasts until the next health issue happens.

Since caring for an older parent may be a new experience for you, guilt can come from an unrealistic concept of caregiving. It can come from trying to answer all of your older parent's demands to make them happy, only to have these attempts fail. It is important to remember you cannot make them happy or fix their limitations or ailments. For some dedicated caregivers, guilt may even be seen as a virtue.

Many times you may go days and days without a break from caregiving, which leaves you feeling exhausted and unloving. You may think or wish you were not the one responsible for their care. And, on occasion, guilt can come from giving into your frustration and anger by yelling. There are numerous ways in which you can experience guilt however, you will need to learn positive self-talk to help overcome the guilt. You will need to tell yourself over and over again that you are doing a fine job and doing your best. *Please remember there is no perfect remedy for you or anyone's caregiving situation.*

Guilt is often the result of how you as a caring woman feel about your personal worth. The issue can become complicated because your earliest foundation of self-esteem was built or neglected by the very person who you are trying to care for now. This person, your parent, knows your weaknesses and failures, and may often remind you of them. Perhaps your parent compares you to your siblings or the adult children of their friends.

The pushing of your hot buttons only increases the difficulty you have in doing what is best for them. Following these encounters, your thoughts may be full of absolute terms, such as should, must, always, never, awful, etc...which only makes you feel defeated

To suppress guilt and other ill feelings can be debilitating. Since these feelings can influence your making wise decisions on behalf of the parent, as well as being detrimental to your health, it is necessary to acknowledge that these feelings are a problem. *Only when you can accept your limitations can you escape from these feelings of misery and guilt.*

Much of the guilt that a caring woman assumes is from attempting to live up to someone else's standards. You are a caring woman, not perfect, just doing the best you can do given the circumstances. And you may need to say to yourself over and over again: "I am a good person." It sounds simplistic however the repetition of positive self-talk actually helps.

Help Relieve the Guilt by Being Informed:

Another cause of guilt and frustration is that you may be dealing with the caregiving situation in small ways rather than looking at the big picture. I call this **the band-aid approach**. It is vital that you plan for the best and worst case scenarios that may arise, tomorrow, next week or in the coming months or years. Caring for your older parent, whose health and safety status is in constant flux, needs a plan. You need to be prepared to discuss the situation realistically with them, if possible, and with other concerned family members.

Do your homework about resources available in the community. By being informed about the options, you can make decisions and plans on what is best for right now. If their health continues to decline and they become more dependent, your plans may need to change. Knowing the various options: home care agencies, alternative living facilities, geriatric physicians and related professionals, you will be able to make informed decisions and wise choices when they are needed.

If all of this feels overwhelming, then a consultation with a geriatric care manager (GCM) can be very beneficial. It can help you understand your parent's options now and in the future. In this way, you will be an informed caring woman and help mitigate the guilt feelings.

> ***Sandy's Story:*** *Sandy G came to see me, as her mother, Ruth, had been asked to leave the assisted living facility (ALF) where she had been living for the past three years. It seems Ruth had maxed out on the amount of services she needed and now required closer supervision, which the ALF was unable to provide. The daughter thought the next step was a nursing home. Not so.*
>
> *Sandy was unaware of the small residential care facilities (RCF) that were available in her community. RCFs are homes located in a residential area, licensed for four to six people, ambulatory or non-ambulatory. RCFs provide all the necessary services for one fee, no add-ons.*
>
> *The particular RCF I recommended had both dementia and hospice waivers, meaning that their staff was trained in handling people with dementia. This meant that Ruth could stay at this RCF until the end of her life. Sandy said the care was excellent and Ruth lived there in a private room for two years before her peaceful death.*

You can alter the causes and patterns of guilt by developing a care plan, and setting boundaries. *(See Chapter 4)*

Chapter #2 - CARING WOMAN TIPS
Develop a (Tentative) Care Plan.

1. **Collect the basic personal information regarding your parent: physical, financial and legal.** Gathering this will serve you well both now and later. Organizing and keeping the relevant information handy will allow you to clarify many issues and help make your caregiving responsibilities run more smoothly.

2. **If possible, have a discussion with your parent**. Approach your parent on a good day and ask what they need. It is not unusual to find that sometimes each of you may see the situation and the needs differently.

3. **Assign duties by people's strengths.** The primary caregiver will be either you or one of your siblings. For now, assign the different duties such as finances, household management, hiring in-home help, etc. *Warning: If your sibling was never good in managing money, do not give him/her charge over the finances!*

4. **Learn the availability of resources in your community, county or state.** Locate resources close to you in your community. Some resources may not be available in your county or state. For example: MediCal (as it is known in California) only pays for nursing home care and a very limited amount for non-nursing home care.

Medicaid (as it is known in the other 49 states) may pay for other kinds of alternative living situations, depending on the state in which your parent resides. You will need to inquire at the local Area Agency on Aging

5. **Keep a notebook or smart phone where you jot down the resources you think are appropriate.** This is for you to keep the names and phone numbers of doctors, attorneys, relatives and close friends who are willing to help out. Write up a list of all your parent's medications including over-the-counter, vitamins and even those expired prescriptions. Make copies of this list to be available when the doctor, paramedics or hospital asks.

6. **Always keep in mind that the bottom-line is your *parent's* safety and security and *your*** peace of mind. Gathering and organizing the necessary physical, financial and legal information early on may seem a tedious task, however this will help when planning for the caregiving days ahead. By being proactive you may head off the surprises and unexpected crises that come along throughout the caregiving journey.

If all of this feels/sounds overwhelming, contact a Geriatric Care Manager through the **Aging Life Care Association**. The ALCA is a national organization of women and men who can assist and guide you through the caregiving process. They are invaluable if you are unfamiliar with resources in your parent's community or live out of the county or state where your parent resides.

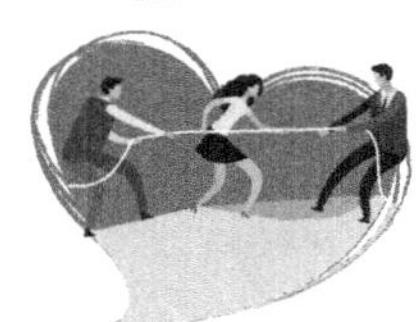

CHAPTER 3:

Sibling Rivalry: Really?

Families are so interesting! Their dynamics can often be incredibly challenging, especially when the whole family is under stress. Families come in many forms: natural, adoptive, step, nuclear, long-distance, estranged, close, dysfunctional, and 57 other varieties. Each and every family is unique in their histories, customs and rituals.

Assumed in family life is caring and loyalty, yet most contain rivalry, competiveness, indifference, alienation and other highly charged emotions. All too often the expectations of what families are supposed to resemble are based on the images of the idealistic families created in sitcoms of the past.

It is important to keep in mind that family relationships can be positive or negative and are usually a mixture of both. Challenges to its balance do not arise just at the time the parent needs care, they are part of the natural evolution of a family's history. Loyalties and alliances among siblings as well as former rivalries may still exist. At the time the older parent needs care, is when the problems and strengths stand out in bold relief. Among adult siblings, the unresolved relationship problems from earlier times are reactivated during any family crisis. The older parent's health situation is such a crisis and disturbs the delicate balance that may have been in place for years.

In reality families are just ordinary individuals who happen to be related by blood, paper or desire. Families are not perfect, nor were they meant to be. The work of learning to get along and compromise may take months, years or a lifetime...or maybe never! This is seen all too clearly when an older parent or favorite relative faces a health crisis or becomes terminally ill. Past hurts, rivalries and the competition for the parent's attention between or among siblings, which may have been dormant for years, can be rekindled. This is called sibling rivalry and can affect the decisions made on behalf of the older adult.

Can this be possible among mature and responsible middle-aged children? If there was rivalry for a parent's approval or affections when the siblings were younger, then more than likely, that rivalry still exists. This is unfinished business. Although seemingly immature behavior, it surfaces during times of stress and the potential loss of the parent. It can be manifested in word or action, subtle or overt, petty or gross, and it is not a pretty sight. This kind of behavior can be detrimental to the appropriate care so necessary for the comfort and safety of the older adult.

The Primary Caregiver and Sibling Rivalry

Regardless of the number of siblings in a family, usually one of them takes on the active role of the primary caregiver—and most times it is a daughter. Maybe she is the sibling who lives closest and has been doing most of the current "checking up." This daughter has been helping to keep the parent in the family home with frequent visits, finding a handyman to fix minor repairs, driving the parent to the doctor, all the while being the constant cheerleader when the parent's everyday issues become overwhelming.

The remaining siblings may maintain contact with periodic visits, or by remembering birthdays or special holidays with gifts and telephone calls.

This is not unusual for many families. Then without warning the older parent has a healthcare crisis: a broken hip, a stroke or advancing signs of dementia. The closest sibling, the Good Daughter, is the one who makes the necessary arrangements. Perhaps she has to find a part-time health aide and convince mother or dad that it is in their best interests to hire someone to come in and assist with medications, cooking and light housekeeping...then she has to convince them to spend the money.

> ***Margery's Story:*** *Margery was one of five siblings, all middle-aged, two sisters and two brothers. June, the 89-year-old mother's, primary medical issue was lung fibrosis and she lived in a city with highly contaminated air. Margery was married to George and lived nearby. Both the doctor and she thought that her mother's health could benefit by moving to an area with cleaner air. Margery did research and found the cleanest air to be in the coastal area of Central California. They moved, leaving the two sisters in the city who could not understand "why their mother was taken away."*

The move was successful as June was able to live alone for several years. Although Margery kept them informed about their mother's health status, the sisters alienated Margery and stopped communicating with her. However, they would occasionally visit their mother, neglecting to tell Margery they were doing so.

When June's ability in remembering her medication and monitoring her oxygen intake became problematic, she moved in with Margery and George. As a retired nurse, Margery was acutely vigilant about her mother's care and agonizingly watched her ever steady decline for the next year.

Finally, June's physician determined she should be on Hospice, where she remained for several months, then went off service, then back on. This off-again-on-again Hospice care went on for over a year and was extremely stressful for Margery. Around this time, she came to realize that maybe the promise she had made to her mother about being able to care for her until the end might not be possible and she began looking into residential care facilities (RCF).

All of this was extremely difficult for Margery, who was continually exhausted. Then she caught a cold that lasted for weeks, and wound up with viral pneumonia. Margery was worn out physically and emotionally and could not get out of bed. ***Her immune system was worn out due to the stress and care of caring for her mother!***

George moved June to a small Hospice-certified RCF where she received excellent care until her death. The down side is that the two sisters continued to ignore Margery, blamed June's decline on the move and did not attend the funeral. They could not emotionally accept the truth of their mother's physical decline.

The up side: George was willing to help, as were the two brothers, one of whom would come one weekend every four months to give Margery and her husband a break. As nice as that was, it was not enough. All of the care, along with the spitefulness of the sisters, increased the stress. This kind of sibling rivalry and behavior causes suffering for all the family!

Margery's sisters were not fair, you say, however, sometimes that is what happens when one of the siblings has to step forward and make the tough decisions.

Sibling rivalry can take many forms, such as an adult son's denial about his mother's mental capacity as she always is "on" when he visits, or a daughter inviting a parent to move in so she can finally win parental approval. There are numerous sibling rivalry scenarios. All can be detrimental to the care so necessary at this time in the frail parent's life. It can also place great stress on the care and decision making efforts of the primary sibling caregiver, **The Good Daughter**.

The following solutions were shared in support groups:

- Your sister gives you unrealistic suggestions on how to improve your mother's care and make it "easier." Barbara, her mother's 24/7 caregiver, was becoming exhausted and Joanne, her sister, was not actively helping, but called constantly to give advice on how to make the job easier. Tired of hearing the advice, Barbara made arrangements to have Joanne watch her mother for a "few" hours. She dropped her mother at her sister's house at 10am and did not return until 6pm. After that Joanne did not offer her unsolicited advice and offered empathy instead. *A lesson learned*.

- Joe, insists that he, his partner and his sister can take care of their father 24/7 working in shifts as Joe does not want to spend his inheritance. It is physically and emotionally demanding work for all. Since the father is on Hospice, the sister enlists the aid of the social worker to mediate a family meeting so a caregiver can be hired for the nighttime care. Although the meeting becomes emotional at times, it does work and a caregiver is hired.

Perhaps, the solution is to be an only child:

- Susan complains about how she and her sister argue constantly over their mother's care, the finances and appropriate health remedies; they cannot seem to agree on anything. In group, Gail, an only child, has been talking about how hard it is to be the one totally responsible for all the details involved in her mother's care. In response to Susan's story, Gail declares, "I think I am *glad* I am an only child."

Lessening the Stress of Sibling Rivalry

Although collaborative efforts among siblings are best, they are not always possible. So what can be done to ease the stress of family caregiving?

First and foremost, have the proper legal documents in place, that is, a Durable Power of Attorney, an Advanced Health Directive, and, if possible, a list of family members and/or friends who will receive particular possessions of the parent(s). Although difficult to discuss failing health and death with an aging parent, it is wise to do so, as it can help prevent misunderstandings with siblings and other family members.

Realize that not every family operates the same way; what works for one family may not work for another. Each and every family member has individual talents and liabilities. Have realistic expectations of what is going to work with siblings based on past behavior. Do not expect a sibling who cannot manage money or neglects their own health to be responsible for the well-being and care of your parent. Give them tasks such as shopping, gardening or errands.

Whatever the family situation, communication is of the utmost importance. If telephone calls or texts are ignored or not returned, **then you still need to keep your siblings informed** about the current situation. Doing this saves aggravation and stress later on as the care increases or upon the death of the older parent.

Depending on the family's dynamics and the issues involved, it may help to have a third party, a geriatric care manager (GCM), social worker, physician, elder law attorney or clergyman mediate a family meeting. This can help in resolving present issues. These kinds of meetings are not intended to settle issues related to past differences. At this time of stress and decision making, past issues need to be set aside as valuable time and energy is wasted on issues that may not be resolved now or ever. With the help of a third party, hopefully siblings will be able to set the past aside temporarily and make their first priority the older parent's care.

Chapter #3 - CARING WOMAN TIPS
Suggestions to help with Sibling Rivalry

1. **Have the appropriate legal documents in place:** A durable power of attorney, an Advanced Health Directive, a will and a list of personal items that are to be left to specific individuals.

2. **Accept siblings** for who they are and expect differences of opinion. Try to respect their perceptions of the situation and find opportunities to compromise.

3. **Be realistic in your expectations.** Allow siblings to help in ways in which they are competent. When assigning chores or duties, do not give the accounting or finances to the sibling who cannot manage money or keep a job.

4. **Be sure to keep family members informed.** Communicate any changes in health or care to all siblings, by email, text or phone. Even if the siblings do not respond, keep them in the caregiving loop. This helps in avoiding misunderstandings now and in the future.

5. **Involve a third party.** If you are having difficulty with a sibling regarding your parent's care, enlist a third party, an individual who is not emotionally involved, to help in resolving the current issues. This individual is not there to solve issues from the past, only to make the best of the present situation.

6. **Remember: The care and safety of the older adult is the primary concern.** Having a settled environment helps lower stress and can make the parent's last days more peaceful.

Chapter 4:

Setting Boundaries in Caregiving

As a caring woman you need to learn to modify expectations, accommodate changes and set boundaries to avoid caregiver burnout. Setting boundaries in the context of caring for your parent means setting boundaries on yourself. Doing this in a healthy way involves balancing love and generosity with self-preservation and knowing that what you are offering is good enough.

Setting boundaries is a firm and caring way of saying "No"; although there may be times when a direct "No" is the only answer to a particular situation. Frequently you will find there is room for adjustment and compromise. The latter lets the parent have some feeling of control over the decisions being made on their behalf.

> ***My Story:*** *When I took care of my dad, it was with the help of my brother, Bob, his partner, Jerry, and Rick the boarder, who lived in my dad's home. Rick was there to drive Pops to the doctor, run errands, fix the evening meal, and as "company." By "company", my dad meant having someone in the house since he did not want to lie dead on the floor for days before someone found him... always practical, that man!*

When Rick moved in, he vowed to be there if and when Pops became ill. This worked for about six years. Pops only chronic illness was high blood pressure. This changed when my dad at 94 began losing his balance, which resulted in many falls. His doctor declared he was having mini-strokes, confined him to bed, and recommended Hospice care. We divided the caregiving into shifts, so we could continue to work, and this would allow Pops to die at home as we had promised.

As my dad's care became more difficult with sundowners and incontinence of bladder and bowel, Rick whined and complained. He began teasing Jerry, who was emotionally fragile, challenged Bob, insulted me and generally became less and less helpful. Jerry was a wonderful caregiver and I did not want him to sink into one of his depressions. Bob, Jerry and I decided Rick had to go or we could easily burn-out with Rick's disruptive jibes.

This is the difficult part: I was the one designated to talk to my dad and feared the ultimatum I had to give him. With my heart pounding, I explained that Rick was being uncooperative, antagonistic and needed to leave. Pops did not want Rick to move out, as he felt sorry for him. So I had to give my dad the unpleasant details of Rick's behavior, which gave him some insight; yet he was not totally convinced. Then I took a deep breath and firmly stated, we cannot deal with Rick's behavior and take good care of you. You have a choice of Bob, Jerry and me or Rick, but not all of us together.

Never in my adult years had I taken the upper hand with my father. Pops, of course, chose the three of us. Although the change was upsetting to my dad, Rick could not stay, as he was causing all of us emotional distress. The caring routine ran more smoothly without Rick so it was worth the temporary angst!

Setting boundaries is not an act of selfishness, but one of caring for your parent, as well as for yourself and other members of your family. Setting boundaries entails your recognizing and accepting of what you realistically can and cannot do and then communicating this to your older parent in an empathetic and sensitive manner. *(See Chapter Five for communication strategies)*

Placement: A Difficult Decision

The caring woman hopes there will not come the time when she will need to make the difficult decision of implementing a different caregiving choice: such as moving the parent from their home. Perhaps a promise was made that the parent could stay at home until the end, however, now you realize that you could not have foreseen the care that might be required to keep that promise.

Has the care the parent requires gone beyond what either you or a paid caregiver can provide? Does the current situation have you lying awake nights worrying about how you are going to manage the increasing care your parent needs along with the responsibilities of your immediate family and/or work? Then it is time to consider an alternative living arrangement.

Moving an older parent, from their home is one of the most difficult decisions you will make in your caregiving journey. Having to make this decision may find you and the parent anxious and unhappy because, chances are, making this kind of decision is not what either of you wanted. Your parent wants to able to live on their own, independently, until they die peacefully in their sleep, which happens only to 6% of people. The caring woman does not want to see her parent become frail and lose control of their physical and mental abilities. Both aging parent and adult child want things to stay the same; it makes caregiving a lot easier. Yet, that is not always possible.

Making lifestyle choices is not easy. Helping an older parent make these choices can be stressful. It may seem as though you are taking over their lives and making the decision for them. However, as the caring woman, you can lessen the stress by making a list of the pros and cons of such a choice and by making a list of your parent's capabilities. This will help you to realize how much help you can give them without jeopardizing your own health and well-being.

None of the choices of alternative living situations will be perfect because this is not *home* or what either of you expected. The parent's life has changed, and their life as they remembered it will never again be the same. At this point in time, what you need to do is focus on making the best choice for the present situation, based on the physical and mental capabilities of your parent.

Perhaps your parent digs in their heels and says they are not moving to "one of those places." Yet, you know that they can no longer live alone, as they frequently miss taking their medications, have fallen numerous times when they forget to use their walker and or they have become incontinent of bladder or bowel. For months you tried numerous paid caregivers and your parent either complains continuously about or to them and they quit or the parent fires them. So for the parent's safety, it is time for a different living arrangement. You may need to engage the assistance of a third party: a physician, lawyer, friend or a GCM to help overcome their resistance.

Think about the safety issues, as they figure prominently in your decision-making process to move a parent. These include missed medications, poor nutrition such as high sodium frozen meals or not eating enough or at all, falling and being unable to get up, dehydration, urinary tract infections (UTIs) [5] from not drinking enough water or not changing their disposable underwear frequently.

Some parents may need to be tricked into moving. Sounds manipulative and devious and yet the move needs to happen. Perhaps, you are going on a trip with your husband or to visit your adult children. Maybe you need to have hip or knee surgery and you do not want to worry about your parent, as it will interfere with the healing and your rehabilitation. These are justifiable reasons for your parent to move. Your parent

---

[5] Having a UTI often exacerbates memory problems; cure the UTI and the increased forgetfulness diminishes.

may need to think that the move is temporary, however, it is not. Having them move to an alternative living arrangement is for their protection and your peace of mind.

There are different types of alternative living arrangements: an assisted living facility (ALF), a residential care facility (RCF) and a skilled nursing facility (SNF). The level of care the older parent requires will determine the choice. *(See Chapter 11 for detailed descriptions.)*

Isabel's Story: *Isabel was a loving, caring daughter. She worked, as did her sister Rose. They wanted to keep their mother Jane at home, which they did with frequent visits and the help of an ongoing parade of paid care providers. However, many times the care providers were unreliable, frequently not showing up on time, and told the sisters that Jane continuously criticized how the meals were cooked and the house was cleaned. The sisters used many home care agencies all with the same results. Although Jane experienced some forgetfulness, she was able to take part in the decision-making process.*

After looking at assisted living facilities near their homes, they found two that allowed a potential resident a trial stay of up to two weeks to see how they liked it. The sisters talked with Jane about the possibility of moving to an ALF, since the home caregiving situation was unstable and frustrating for all involved. The mother expressed reluctance and yet she was exhausted from the unreliability of the paid care providers who did not do things the way she liked. Maybe, the sisters suggested, she would be willing to give the ALF a two week trial? Jane agreed.

Well, surprise, surprise, Jane really enjoyed the social aspect of having meals with other residents and having her apartment cleaned regularly. Jane seemed to thrive in the new environment with its social activities and outings, things she did not have isolated in her house with a paid care provider. Also available was extra care when and if she needed it in the future.

As a caring woman having to make the decision to move a parent from their home is not what you wanted to do; no caring woman does. Yet, the many changes in health and family circumstances often necessitate lowering expectations and setting boundaries.

You can help yourself by involving other family members and reassuring your older parent that you will not abandon them. Tell your parent that their health, safety and well-being are of utmost importance. Discuss your concerns with them and why you feel the present situation is not working. You may be surprised to find that your aging parent has been giving the situation a lot of thought and may be willing to accommodate your needs. Parents do not like to feel alienated. They want and need to know you care. When you set boundaries, not from frustration and anger, but from a mature stance based on knowing your personal strengths and limitations, your parent will usually respond positively.

Guidelines to Help Set Boundaries
Chapter #4 - CARING WOMAN TIPS

1. **Respect the dignity of your aging parents when responding to their requests.** Tell them you are thinking about their future and how best to fulfill their living requirements based on their health and safety. Ask them what they think would work best before offering your opinion. You can suggest the options available in their community.

2. **Evaluate your parent's limitations.** If you find your parent expects too much of you, then you will have to weigh which requests are the most important. For example: Do you really need to visit them every day if at home or in a care facility? If they are at home and their safety is at risk then you may need to hire someone to visit daily.

   If they under the care of a reliable facility, it is often better to limit your visits to two or three times a week. This gives your parent time to adjust to the new living arrangement.

3. **Accept your limitations.** If you do too much, then become exhausted providing these services, then who will help when assistance is really needed? Remember that too often the caregiver becomes ill or dies first.

4. **Agree to provide only those services you can manage gracefully and with good humor.** Get others to assist you with some of the chores. Help provided out of guilt only leaves both you and your parents feeling frustrated. When asking for help from others be specific about your needs and times/days to visit, bring a meal, or visit for a couple of hours so you can have a break or do errands.

5. **Be firm in your decisions.** If you consider a request unreasonable or unmanageable, explain your position and make alternative suggestions. Don't feel like you have to continually justify yourself with a parent or other family member. If you, the doctor or the hospital discharge planner tells you that your parent can no longer live alone: **pay heed**. As long as they are alive, their health and safety are your primary concerns.

6. **Realize that you are not responsible for their happiness.** Many older adults have difficulty accepting the limitations that accompany aging, and look for someone else to blame for their distress. Accepting the blame and the guilt for your parent's dissatisfaction does not help anyone. Consider their lifetime personality: always a complainer, always stubborn, always blaming? Those traits are not going to change.

7. **Do not promise your parent that they can stay at home till the end.** If you parent asks not to be put in a nursing home, think about your answer. The time may come when caregiving becomes so physically beyond you or a home health aide's capabilities and your parent's physical or medical needs that placement is the only way to continue. So the best response is to tell your parent you will care for them as long as you are able. This gives you an out if the care gets beyond your abilities and will lessen your guilt.

8. **Let your parents know you care, even though you may not always meet all of their requests.** Show your affection spontaneously by sharing special times, by touching, hugging, calling to share news, writing brief notes, or bringing them a flower from your garden.

Chapter 5:

Communication: Finding Common Ground

What is good communication? It is getting a message across between two or more people, so each can understand the other's needs, desires and feelings. The goal of communication is to achieve some kind of unity – a oneness of understanding. This can become extremely difficult when a caring woman attempts to discuss personal concerns with an increasingly frail parent. However, good, clear communication with an older parent is essential, if positive interaction, understanding and acceptance are desired.

Quite often problems arise, when you try to have the parent do things the way you think is best, and much time may be spent trying to convince them. Your older parent in turn wants to convince you that their way is best. Very quickly there is frustration, teeth-gritting and deadlock.

Communication between an older parent and a caring woman can also be tricky due to a variety of physical and emotional reasons: hearing loss, denial, fear, depression, attitudes, life experiences, etc. The challenge of having a productive conversation becomes greater as the amount of care the older adult needs increases.

Attempt to look beyond the wrinkles, gray hair and frailty of mind or body and remember the parent's unique qualities both the positive and negative ones. It is important to keep in mind that the older parent has been independent for years and having to relinquish even a little bit of their autonomy can be very difficult. In fact, it can signify that it is the beginning of the end, which can be extremely troubling to your parent and makes them more keenly aware of their mortality.

To communicate effectively, you must know who and where you are at this moment in the caregiving journey and where the older parent is. Where the parent is right now is brand new for them. They are losing their independence: control over their minds or bodies, their decisions and their checkbook. For a moment put yourself in their place and think of how you would feel if you were unable to manage your money, shop or cook your own meals. Being unable to accomplish all of the personal things you managed for years is very disheartening.

Most adult children find it difficult to talk with their parent about the things that might be needed at the end of life: finances, living arrangements, or declining health and the care that may entail. These issues can make for an extremely uncomfortable conversation. Sometimes a parent may think your interest is for personal gain when you want to discuss their financial situation. They may not want to talk about declining health as it means becoming dependent on you or having to find another living arrangement and move from their cherished home. And for you it is painful to think about watching your once capable parent's declining physical health or advancing dementia and not know how much care may be needed or how long the caregiving journey will last.

Listening for *THAT* Opportunity

Learning about a parent's finances and health care wishes can help prevent serious problems later. You will want to know their desires and concerns. If the older parent suffers a stroke or becomes incapacitated due to dementia, you will need to know where the important documents are located. Talking with your parent now, and having a plan in place, even if it only tentatively addresses these issues, can make everyone involved feel more at ease.

Since these kinds of conversations are so often filled with hot-button potential, how do you start? Perhaps your parent has already mentioned some issues that pertain to aging and you may have brushed them aside as these issues made you feel uncomfortable. Who wants to talk with their parent about the parent becoming incapacitated or dying? Yet, when a parent brings up a subject related to aging, it can be exactly the opening you need.

Listen carefully to your parent. Maybe in casual conversation they have mentioned a friend that recently had a health crisis or one who has died. Perhaps your parent has been thinking about some personal issues and is now ready to talk about them. If you brushed their comments aside previously because you were uncomfortable, then you missed a good opportunity. Next time an issue related to aging comes into the conversation, pursue it gently and slowly. You may be surprised to find out that your parent has already given a lot of thought to the future.

If your parent remains reluctant to talk about such things, there are other ways to begin this discussion. Think about the issues you want to bring up then add your own spin to the dialogue. For example, ask for their advice, listen to them closely, ask questions, use specific statements rather than general ones and voice your personal concerns for their safety and well-being. Maybe you found an interesting newspaper or magazine article about aging or a well-known celebrity of their era who just died. This is an opportunity!

Sometimes even the most creative way of bringing up the subjects that pertain to your parent's future may not be successful. If this happens, then step back and approach these issues another way or at a later date. Allowing the older adult some time to mull over and react to the seriousness of your concerns is important. As you know from other communication challenges with friends or in business, major issues are seldom settled the first time or in a single discussion.

Are you experiencing discomfort discussing these issues? Perhaps you are in a hurry to settle the important issues and be done with it. Often our discomfort with these topics shines through and transfers to the parent, creating anxiety and too often wasted efforts and fruitless negotiation.

You can be assertive without being aggressive. Trying to inflict your ideas and solutions on your parent will leave them feeling helpless and powerless. By being gently assertive you can tell the parent what you need to have happen while taking into account what they need.

Since many of the aging issues that need to be discussed are emotionally charged, or in some cases may be considered off limits by your parent, then it may be easier to have a third party run interference. That is a person who is not emotionally involved, such as a doctor, financial advisor, attorney, an impartial relative (maybe a son-in-law), a friend or a geriatric care manager [6].

> ***Katherine's Story:*** *Katherine attended a support group and in it expressed her frustration with her mother, who lived out of state. Although her sister, Anne, lived near her mother, neither one could get Mom to do anything that was suggested, such as hire someone to come a few hours a couple of days a week to run errands, drive Mom to frequent doctor visits and to clean the house. According to Katherine, Mom was living in her home with the curtains drawn, eating frozen meals, and not leaving except to go to the doctor by taxi. The sisters had tried and tried for many months to have Mom get some in-home help to no avail. Katherine told the group that she was worried for her mother's safety as her mother had previously experienced bouts of depression.*
>
> *The group facilitator suggested contacting a geriatric care manager (GCM)* [6]*, a neutral third party, to pay Mom a visit. Katherine was given names of GCMs who lived*

---

[6] *Geriatric Care Manager: see Resources for description and contact information.*

in her Mom's city and one was hired. The GCM visited Katherine's mom several times and accomplished what the sisters had been trying to do for months! Katherine was extremely pleased with the results, as it meant both sisters were assured of their mother's safety and well-being for the present. Mom had confidence in the GCM, so if further changes became necessary, the GCM could be called upon to help negotiate and locate the appropriate resources.

For some reason many older parents resent having their adult children giving them advice. Maybe it is that the caring woman behaves as though the parent is their child instead of having ever been a capable adult. Also some older parents are in denial and do not want to think about health issues, as it means losing their power and gaining on the end of life. These are the difficult conversations that often end up hitting a brick wall or a stalemate. Frequently a third party, a son or son-in-law is a good start. Many older adults think that the man knows best. Every family is different, so think through what may be the best approach for your situation.

Always keep their values, concerns, likes and dislikes in mind. As an example, consider the food they like and even the way it is presented.

Ellen's Story: *Ellen's mother, Betty, was living in her own home with the help of a paid caregiver who came in three times a week to cook, do laundry and light housekeeping.*

Betty complained regularly that the she did not like the caregiver's cooking and wanted another caregiver someone who knew how to cook. To Ellen, it looked like a balanced meal, with the food items Betty liked. What was there to complain about? Well, it took several weeks of gentle questioning for Ellen to discover that her mother did not like the way the caregiver cooked the vegetables. They were prepared tender-crisp and Betty liked them almost mushy. Also, Betty said the food did not taste the same. After researching the medications Betty was taking, Ellen discovered that two of them had the possibility of altering the taste of food and drink. What may seem like a small issue to a caring woman can be a large issue to the older parent, as they often have little say over important, everyday choices.

Continue to remember that having these discussions and knowing your parent's wishes is vitally important to their health and well-being. It will also bring comfort to you both should the caregiving circumstances change to the need for more care, someone to manage financial matters, or even a move to another living situation. When your parent is gone, it will be easier for you to settle their estate and move forward, knowing that you followed their wishes and met their needs to the best of your ability.

Honor the older parent as an adult with their own way of handling things.

Remember that they were brought up in a different time where the cost of hiring help was not as expensive, so allow them to have their say. Treat them with genuine respect in word and action. In spite of their physical or mental decline, let them have dignity. Do not treat them as though they are not capable of making decisions. The older parent does not have as many choices as they used to have. It may take time to reach a mutual understanding, so please be patient.

Chapter 5: CARING WOMAN TIPS
Suggestions for Better Communication

1. **Ask Open Questions.** Asking only questions that have yes or no answers or could be answered with a single word usually stops the flow of communication. For example: "How was your visit to the doctor today?" could be answered with an uninformative "Fine." Instead ask: "What did the doctor say about your new heart medication?"

2. **Self-Disclosure:** How do we get parents to talk about themselves—to really express their feelings? This is difficult for many older parents. If we want them to open up then we must self-disclose. Tell them *your* feelings. For example: "I'm worried about your weight loss. You may not think it's important, but I am losing sleep over it and would feel so much better if you would tell your doctor."

3. **Acceptance:** When your parent complains about physical ailments or lack of attention, don't judge. Hear what they say. Validate where they are. For example: "Yes, it must be terribly frustrating to be unable to do what you want." If your parent says something you disagree with, it can help to say "I hear what you said only I don't agree with you." Don't argue or confront. It will get you nowhere and just leads to mutual frustration.

4. **Ask Questions:** Encourage talking. So many times we assume things about what the parent says. Often what they are saying is a cover-up for their feelings of inadequacy, loss of control or fear. Paraphrase what they are saying with "I" statements. For example: "I hear you saying you do not want a stranger in the house and yet I am concerned about you being here by yourself all day, every day."

5. **Verbal Reassurance:** Very often service providers just do their job and see older people as a group and therefore do not see them as individuals. Perhaps older parents' behaviors and reactions appear to be the same because they are having the same feelings about coping with their losses, vulnerability and increasing frailty. Try to see them as an individual with the same personality, needs and desires they had when they were younger and in better health. It helps when the caring daughter and other family members

reassure the parent and say, "I'm listening," or "I care," or "I love you."

6. **Silence:** Sometimes just sitting and watching a favorite television show without talking is enough. Silence can be as eloquent as touching. All of these say you care. The idea of forcing communication can be self-defeating. Yet, often real communication takes place when you are in the process of doing some other activity with your parent.

7. **Assertive Listening:** Are you meeting too much resistance from your parent? Then perhaps it is time for assertive communication. This is expressing your concerns while acknowledging theirs, and exploring what needs to be accomplished for their safety and well- being. Hopefully you will find common ground thereby avoiding unnecessary conflict. This is different from being aggressive and rolling over the parent's wishes which will only impede what you want to accomplish and thwart successful communication.

8. **Saying "No":** When you even think of saying "No," you probably feel guilty; yet, boundaries need to be set. When setting boundaries, offer alternatives. For example: If you can't take your parent shopping or to the doctor, offer them suggestions for alternative transportation, like a

senior center bus service. Telling them that you will be glad to make those arrangements. Then they will know that not going to the doctor is their choice and not your fault.

9. **Be a Good Listener:** Listen attentively with interest and intelligent reflection, particularly when it is most boring. Encourage your parent to talk about themselves, their past successes and accomplishments, no matter how big or how small. Remember that more often than not, they do not have much excitement in their everyday lives.

10. **Make Time for Good, Productive Communication:** You can be extremely busy, taking care of your loved one's constant needs, as well as those of your other family members and yourself. Yet, meaningful communication takes time, lots of time, and patience and caring. Try to make special time to sit with your parent quietly, perhaps with a cup of tea and a snack. It will create a special memory for you both.

Chapter 6:

Avoiding Caregiver Burnout

Although caregiving can be rewarding and bring satisfaction, it can wear you out physically, mentally and emotionally to the point where you literally burnout... meaning you cannot keep up the frantic pace, can no longer function and can become ill. The stressors pile up: changes in family dynamics, tension with siblings, financial concerns, losing focus at work. Now add into that stress bomb the workload of caring for an older parent who may have several chronic illnesses and/or dementia. All of this spinning around in your head becomes overwhelming and just adds to the existing stress of daily living. Although you know you are in for the long haul, you don't know how long a haul it will be.

Many caring women discover that the stress outweighs the satisfaction or the fulfillment. Sometimes the emotional stress of providing care tends to be greater than the physical or financial costs, since caregivers frequently give up personal renewal time. As result of multiple responsibilities, caregiving can cause serious illness, depression or even death to the caring family member. Known as **Caregiver Burnout**, it affects at least 44% of family caregivers. [7] Ready for some good news? There are things you can do to prevent it.

Even though a caregiver may think, "Why do I have to do all the work?" or "How long will I have to do this?" generally they don't actually ask others for help nor do they seek out community resources. A caring woman may sacrifice a job, hobbies, social events, vacations and/or privacy. When concerned friends question these sacrifices or make suggestions to get help, a caregiver may reply, "Well, my parent (mother, father, grandparent) took care of me, now it's my turn to care for them." That may be how you feel or believe, but as mentioned previously, taking care of an older parent is vastly different from caring for a child.

Instead of gratitude, a litany of complaints about what is and isn't right or what needs to be done, or detailed descriptions of physical ailments may be the caring woman's only feedback. If the parent suffers from dementia, then it will be the same questions repeated over again while you are trying to get the chores finished. So the idea of taking personal time is usually at the bottom of the adult daughter's to-do list. The health concerns and well-being of the older parent often depend on the ability of the caregiver to handle all the details.

Keeping track of multiple medications, doctor appointments, housekeeping, laundry, marketing, cooking and the personal care needs of the older parent is almost an impossible task. Doing all that while watching the older

---

[7] *National Alliance on Caregiving &AARP Public Health Institute*, 2015

parent's memory and personality slip away due to dementia, added to the realization that they are rapidly approaching the end of life, can be emotionally devastating and completely overwhelming.

Having to face the excessive physical demands, as well as emotional demands, makes you vulnerable to serious illness, such as:

- stroke
- heart attack
- depression
- alcohol abuse
- abuse or neglect of the older adult

Caring women often find that the dominant element in their caregiving is not the particular chores they perform, but the continual sense of responsibility for their parent's emotional state. From personal experience and many years of consulting with families, I am here to say caregiving is not a job to be taken lightly. The mood swings and emotional ups and downs are not to be ignored. Look over the following checklist. Which ones are affecting you?

Common Signs and Symptoms of Stress:

- [ ] Feeling tired and run down
- [ ] Difficulty falling asleep or staying asleep
- [ ] Overreacting to small mistakes or omissions

- [ ] Trouble concentrating
- [ ] Becoming increasingly resentful
- [ ] Feeling tired and exhausted all the time
- [ ] Drinking, smoking or eating more
- [ ] Cutting back on or eliminating hobbies and leisure time

If you answer "Yes" to more than two of these, you are officially stressed and may find yourself a candidate for burnout. [8]

Common Signs and Symptoms of Caregiver Burnout:

- [ ] You do not have the same energy you used to enjoy.
- [ ] You do not recover from exhaustion, even after sleep.
- [ ] You catch colds frequently and cannot seem to get over them.
- [ ] You neglect your own needs, either because you are too busy or don't care.
- [ ] Your entire life revolves around caregiving and yet, it gives you little satisfaction.

---

[8] Reread Margery's story in Chapter 3

- ☐ You have trouble relaxing, even when help is available.

- ☐ You feel helpless and hopeless, and do not see an end.

Do not ignore these signs! Caregiver stress and burnout put your health at risk and affects your ability to provide care. This can hurt both you and your older parent. You, as a caring woman, need care, too. So remember to give yourself some "you" time. You will have more energy and more patience if you do.

Karen's Story: *Karen's mother, Hazel, began having small strokes and was told she could no longer live alone. Although, there were four siblings, Hazel came to live with Karen and her husband, Fred, in a two-bedroom mobile home. Karen was insistent that she could do it all since finances were limited. As Hazel's dementia progressed, Hazel became fearful of water and fought getting into the shower. It was suggested that Karen ask one of her siblings for help, or at least help by paying to hire a professional to help her mother shower.*

"Oh, they can't afford it," Karen declared. Finally after many months of suggestions from support group members, a female bath aide was hired to come twice a week. What a difference! The woman cajoled and soothed Hazel and the shower was no longer a fight. This went on for two years....with Karen becoming even more exhausted as her mother began having sundowners.

One day, Fred called in tears, saying that Karen was near death, as she had ignored her stomach pains and her gallbladder was grossly infected. She had sepsis and her immune system was weak from the constant stress of caring for her mother. It took many weeks for Karen to recover. Her doctor emphatically told Karen and Fred: "No more caregiving." That meant placement. Well, surprise, surprise, the siblings stepped in and each contributed to the cost of a residential care facility (RCF). Karen had not asked her siblings previously, as she did not want to impose "her troubles" on them. As many dutiful daughters do, she really believed she could do it all because she loved her mother and wanted to take care of her until the end. Unfortunately, that is not always realistic.

Taking Care of YOU.

You cannot stop the effect that chronic illness or progressive disease has on your parent. However, there is a great deal you can do to take responsibility for your own personal well-being in order to have your own needs met.

Too often, attitudes and beliefs form personal barriers that stand in the way of caring for yourself. Negative self-talk such as "There is no way I can find the time to exercise" or "I'll just have a bowl of cereal for dinner," becomes the new normal. Not exercising, not eating well and not taking care of yourself may even be a lifelong pattern, as taking care of others can be an easier option. Think about this: If you become ill or die, then what good are you to your aging loved one?

Because we tend to base our behavior on our thoughts and beliefs, if we think negatively, then the mind believes it. Caregivers attempt to do what cannot be done; to control what cannot be controlled. Does everything done for your parent need to be perfect? Do minor chores need to be done at exactly the same time every day? You are attempting the impossible: to be *all things* to *everybody* in your life. It cannot be done.

A Prescription: Give yourself some time **every day** to do something you enjoy, even if it is only 15 or 20 minutes. In that brief period, you can "escape" and you will have something to look forward to tomorrow.

Chapter # 6 Caring Woman Tips
Tips to Help Avoid Caregiver Burnout

1. **Ask for Help.** Do not expect family and friends to step up to the plate without you asking them. They may think you do not need help since you look like you are doing a good job, no matter how stressed you are. So speak up and give them a specific task, even it is only a simple one. Would you pick up Mom's Rx at the store? Would you stay with Mom while I go on an errand? Can you contribute to the cost of a part-time home health aide for Dad?

2. **Share Some of the Responsibilities.** One family member should not have to do everything. So be willing to relinquish some of the responsibility aka control. Do not try to control every aspect of care. Micromanaging and doing everything your way is a turn off to anyone who would like to help.

3. **Give Yourself a Break.** This may seem impossible with all that needs to be accomplished, however taking some time for you every day is a necessity. A *minimum* is 30-minutes a day. Stop, take a deep breath, go outside, or turn on some music and just sit down. Yes, the dishes will wait as will the floors.

4. **Find Local Resources to Help.** There are many resources to help that may be free or low-cost.

Call the Area Agency on Aging, Alzheimer's Association, Family Caregiver Network, or your local Adult Day Care Center. Some agencies receive grants that offer limited funds to help pay for respite care. *(See Resources to Help on page 165.)*

5. **Join a Support Group.** These groups are a safe place where you can share your feelings and frustrations with others who have similar situations and are experiencing many of the same feelings. Get tips from others and learn about resources in your community that can help you and your parent.

6. **Take Care of Yourself.** You are your loved one's best asset. Protect you!

- **I have the right to take care of myself.** This is not an act of selfishness. It will give me the capability of taking better care of my loved one.

---

9 Adapted from ***When An Aging Loved One Needs Care***, Ron DelBene with Mary and Herb Montgomery, Upper Room Books, Nashville, Tennessee

- **I have the right to seek help from others,** even though my parent may object. I recognize the limits of my own endurance and strength.

- **I have the right to maintain areas of interest in my own life that do not include the person I care for,** just as I would if he/she were healthy. I know that I do everything that I reasonably can for this person, and I have the right to do somethings just for myself.

- **I have the right to get angry, feel sad or hurt,** and occasionally express other difficult feelings.

- **I have the right to reject any attempt by my parent (either conscious or unconscious) to manipulate me** through guilt, anger or sadness.

- **I have the right to receive consideration, affection, forgiveness and acceptance** from my parent for what I do as long as I offer these qualities in return.

- **I have the right to take pride in what I am accomplishing** and to applaud the courage it has sometimes taken to meet the needs of my parent/ loved one.

- **I have the right to protect my individuality and my right to make a life for myself** that will sustain me in the time when my parent/loved one no longer needs my help.

I have the right to expect and demand that, as continuing strides are made in finding resources to aid physically and mentally impaired older persons, similar strides will be made toward aiding and supporting caregivers.

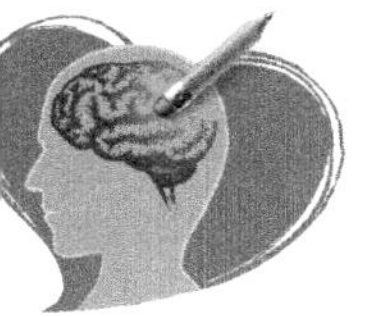

Chapter 7:

Dementia: Symptoms and Treatments.

This chapter has a lot of information and may seem somewhat over-whelming, however be patient and read through it. You will be glad you did.

Your parent and, for that matter, many older adults, are fearful of losing their memory. In our country alone, 5.7 million people are living with Alzheimer's disease [10], which is only one form of dementia. Is it any wonder then that older adults and their family members are concerned that dementia may affect them? Yet, too often caring women pass over the symptoms of forgetfulness in their older loved ones as just being part of the aging process. Not so. Despite popular belief, memory loss is not a normal part of aging. All memory loss has a cause; it does not just happen because one is a certain age.

The mental ability of your older parent can vary from day to day for various reasons: they may not be feeling well, have possible side effects from a new medication or from being lonely and isolated. Walking into a room and then forgetting why you are there is not dementia- it is called *benign senescence*. This is ordinary forgetting because you are busy

---

[10] *Alzheimer's Association* 2018

and are thinking of the next thing you have to accomplish. The serious kind, as an elderlaw attorney said many years ago "is not when you forget your keys, it is when you forget what your keys are for."

However, if your older parent is exhibiting signs of memory loss, confusion or disorientation more and more frequently, it is time to consider that these behaviors may be the early signs of dementia. Consider these symptoms:

- Do they repeatedly ask the same question?
- Are bills unpaid?
- Is food in the fridge becoming moldy?
- Is their personal hygiene being neglected?

These are just a few signs of the early stages of dementia or depression and, in some cases the early stages of dementia can mimic depression.

For your older parent, their mental health, forgetfulness and/or loss of memory are touchy and sensitive subjects. Although your concerns for their safety and well-being are justified, discussing it with them does not mean your suggestions or ideas will be met with agreement. When someone is acting in ways that do not make sense, our tendency is to carefully explain the situation, calling on their sense of appropriateness to get them to agree. However with dementia, there may not be rational thinking, so expecting your older parent to agree to your logical arguments is often futile.

As a caring woman it helps to understand that our personality does not change with age. It is the one constant throughout one's lifetime. Illness, medication and/or mental decline can exaggerate lifelong personality traits, good and bad. What you may observe or think of as a personality change in your older parent is not due to aging but to some physical, mental or emotional change.

Neither does intelligence decline with age. Creativity and judgment (wisdom) usually *increase* with age. Too often in our present day culture, older adults are thought to be lesser people as they become a "certain age." Even today the terms "old timer's disease" or" senility" are often used in referring to an older adult who may be experiencing forgetfulness or unusual behavior. Since senility is not a disease, this term is erroneous and obsolete.

Memory problems that cause changes in behaviors or personality may be a form of brain disease called dementia. Dementia is the contemporary term for a group of symptoms applied to a person who is exhibiting memory loss, confusion, declining problem-solving capabilities, poor judgment skills and language deficits. Some symptoms of dementia are reversible while others are not. Listed below are examples of the irreversible and reversible causes of dementia.

Irreversible	**Reversible** [11]
Alzheimer's Disease	Depression
Multi-infarct Dementia	Medication Interactions
Frontotemporal Dementia	Vitamin B12 Deficiency
Parkinson's Disease	Infections (UTIs)
Lewy Body Disease	Hormonal or Thyroid Problems
Huntington's Disease	Dehydration/Malnutrition

Serious — HEAD INJURY — Minor

Understand that dementia is not a normal part of aging. All serious memory loss has a cause. Dementia can happen to anyone at any age. Though Alzheimer's disease is the most prevalent cause of dementia in later life, there are other conditions with a variety of causes that produce similar symptoms *(see Dementia list above)*. Some of these conditions respond to treatment, while others are irreversible.

Dementia can go undetected for months or even years, often begins slowly, and gradually worsens. If your parent is asking the same questions repeatedly, becoming lost in familiar places, becoming disoriented about time, people and places, neglecting personal hygiene and safety, then there is a strong possibility that they are suffering from dementia. The older adult does not need to exhibit all of these symptoms at once as having only one of these can indicate dementia.

[11] *Alzheimer's Association 2018*

Even with the increasing awareness of dementia, many family physicians put off a diagnosis and dismiss the symptoms as mild memory impairment rather than give a more comprehensive diagnosis to the patient and family members. If this diagnosis does not satisfy what you have been observing in your older adult's behaviors, then look for another physician, preferably a neurologist, who is more familiar with the various types of dementia and its causes.

Another alternative is to find a university or teaching hospital that has a Brain and Memory Center located near where your parent lives. An evaluation from one of these centers is more comprehensive and involves a thorough physical, neurological, and psychiatric examination and usually suggestions for treatment and care.

Vivian's Story: *Vivian's widowed father, Harold, lived with her due to his physical challenges and financial limitations. During the day, he watched a lot of television. Vivian noticed that, increasingly, her father became confused between reality and what he observed on the television. At one point, he came into the kitchen saying, "Did you know that Frank Sinatra is President of the United States?" Other times he made up erratic stories about people and events in the distant past. At first she thought this confusion might be due to his new heart medication. Vivian had worked in a doctor's office and understood what can happen when an older adult begins a new medication.*

They went to Harold's doctor, who gave him the mini-mental exam and declared him okay. In her frustration, she told the doctor, "You're not living with him!" which just got her "a look" from the doctor.

Attending a support group, Vivian learned about the comprehensive evaluation given at a nearby Brain and Memory Center, with most of the cost covered by Medicare and his supplemental insurance. She made the appointment and was told he ***did*** *have multi-infarct dementia, due to many small strokes. Harold was given medications to help with the hallucinations and erratic behaviors.*

By taking a class from the Alzheimer's Association and participating in a support group, Vivian learned better ways of communicating with her father which lessened his confrontational behaviors and also had him attend an Adult Day Center three days a week, where he could find both physical and mental stimulation.

Alzheimer's Disease

The two most frequent causes of irreversible memory impairment are Alzheimer's disease and multi-infarct dementia, sometimes called vascular dementia. Although the causes of Alzheimer's disease are unknown, it is a degenerative disorder that is characterized by a specific set of physiological changes in the brain.

Nerve fibers surrounding the brain's memory center become tangled and information is no longer carried to or from the brain *(the brain begins to look like a plastic pot scrubber)*. Symptoms, such as forgetfulness and mood swings begin slowly and become steadily worse, making early detection difficult, especially because older adults suffering from dementia lose their abilities at different rates.

Sadly, at the present time, there is no cure for this devastating disease. There are medications that claim to slow the progress, however they do not work for everyone. Although there is not a medical cure, there are ways of helping you and other family members to better handle the difficult behaviors the disease produces. Education and assistance are available through the Alzheimer's Association, free or at low cost. Another resource is Adult Day Centers that offer daytime care with structured activities. Taking your older adult to one of these centers can give you and other family caregivers a much needed break and respite while offering your loved one stimulation and socialization.

Today, a victim of Alzheimer's, or one of the several other dementing diseases, have choices, however the family is still the main caregiving support to these older adults. Most family members want to care for their aging loved ones, and feel guilty when they have to place them in a facility when the care becomes too difficult.

A Brief Personal Story: *Many years ago my maternal grandmother began having memory lapses, which doctors at that time referred to as senility. As the months passed, she began wandering and hitching rides to our home 15 miles away. My grandfather, who had heart problems, could not contain her at home nor give her the care she needed. My mother tried, but found it not workable,* *especially when my grandmother became incontinent and belligerent. My mother finally had to place her in a facility. They had been very close all their lives, so this was an incredibly difficult decision.*

This scenario is played out over and over again even today: frustration that we want to be able to do it all topped with guilt, because we cannot. Some things do not change.

Nancy Regan referred to Alzheimer's disease as the "long goodbye." Because there is natural sadness and frustration associated with caring for an older parent with dementia, it is a **necessity** that the caring woman attends an appropriate support group where she can share her sorrow and the gradual loss of the loved one.

In a support group, participants learn from other caregivers better ways to cope, as well as having the reassurance that they are not alone with their frustrations and grief. Believe or not, there is joy and laughter to be found there with others who are traveling the same road as you.

Multi-infarct Dementia

Multi-infarct dementia is the second most common type of dementia and can be the result of a series of small strokes or TIAs (transient ischemic attacks), which damage or destroy the brain tissue. The location in the brain where the strokes occur and the severity of the strokes are what determine the seriousness of the problem and the symptoms.

The symptoms usually begin suddenly, and may include weakness in an arm or leg, slurred speech and dizziness, and do not last more than a few days. The person may improve for a short period of time until the next small stroke and further decline. Several TIAs may occur before any residual symptoms are noticed. In the beginning most TIAs do not show up on an MRI.

In addition to confusion and dificulty with recent memory, symptoms may include:

- getting lost in familiar places
- wandering
- incontinence of bladder or bowel
- inappropriate emotions such as laughing or crying at the wrong time
- difficulty following instructions
- difficulty handling money.

While no treatment can undo the damage that has been done, physicians believe that it is important to prevent further strokes for people with multi-infarct dementia by controlling their high blood pressure, monitoring and treating high cholesterol and diabetes, and helping them to stop if they smoke.

Additionally, there are some 100 other problems or conditions that can mimic dementia, including:

- a minor head injury (from a fall)
- high fever

- poor nutrition
- dehydration
- thyroid or hormonal imbalances
- UTI (urinary tract infection)
- adverse drug reactions
- depression

Lena's Story: *Lena's mother, Rosa, had mild dementia and for the past two years had been living comfortably in an assisted living facility. She had her own apartment with meals, housekeeping and activities as part of her daily routine. Then out-of- the-blue, Rosa's mild and cooperative manner changed dramatically.*

She was becoming quarrelsome with the facility's staff and uncooperative with Lena and her sister. More and more frequently, Lena was receiving phone calls from the facility's staff describing her mother's agitated behavior. She was also told that Rosa might have to leave the facility and find another place to live, as she was being disruptive to the other residents. Lena took her mother to the family physician and he told her that probably the dementia was just progressing and gave Rosa a prescription for an anti-anxiety medication. The behaviors stayed the same.

With some online research, Lena wondered if the changes in her mother's behavior might be the result of diminished activity of Rosa's thyroid gland. Lena took her mother to an endocrinologist, who changed her thyroid medication to no avail. After several fruitless visits to other recommended physicians, Lena finally took her mother to a university teaching hospital and, there, the physicians found that Rosa's parathyroid gland, a very small gland near the thyroid, was not functioning properly. That was treated and Rosa behaviors mellowed.

It is hard to believe that something so small could make such big changes in behavior, but it did. Lena trusted her instincts and pursued them to resolution.

Depression

Depression can be a serious problem for older adults, and its symptoms often mimic the early stages of dementia, including poor hygiene, difficulty remembering and denial. Research [12] shows that as 15% to 27% of older adults experience some depressive symptoms. However, compare that number to the statistics of depression in family caregivers, and the symptoms dramatically increase, with up to 87% suffering from chronic fatigue, feelings of helplessness and resentment.

Many older adults are reluctant or unable to express unpleasant emotions and/or tend to bury painful feelings. As a result, depression in older adults is manifested in memory problems, slowed cognitive processing and poor decision making. Sometimes it is expressed in an inordinate concern

---

[12] *Family Caregiver Alliance* 2002

for medical problems or constant complaining about daily life to you and others who will listen.

Loneliness, isolation and a loss of purpose can be another cause of depressive symptoms. Some older adults experience several losses that occur in a short period of time. They may suffer the loss of a spouse, siblings, friends, pets, finances, housing and physical abilities. Sometimes these losses come together or one after another, but all loss creates some degree of grief. The more serious the loss, the longer the grief lasts.

Following loss, a person can be expected to exhibit a variety of responses: shock, denial, anger, sadness, guilt and finally acceptance. If these responses are blocked or ignored, the person becomes "stuck" and is unable to resolve the grief. If this happens, significant depression can follow, and may require professional treatment with medication or counseling.

Note that most anti-depressants can take up to six weeks before one sees improvement and many older adults become impatient and quit the medication before it has time to work. This can be very frustrating for the caring woman who is trying so hard to make her older parent feel better.

The first step in coping with depression is to recognize and acknowledge the symptoms. Many older adults find this troubling as they associate any mental illness with craziness or insanity and fear they might be "put away."

Often, depression is masked by other chronic physical problems, making an accurate diagnosis difficult.

Seek Help with Symptoms of Dementia

With so many causes of dementia, it is of upmost importance to obtain an accurate diagnosis preferably from a physician who understands the aging process. If your parent's regular physician is not up to speed on dementia, then seek the help of a neurologist or geriatrician. They are more willing to take the time to determine the symptoms of dementia or depression by looking at the whole person, not just the physical ailments. If you unable to find such a physician, contact the Alzheimer's Association for a referral to a Brain & Memory Center, so your older parent can obtain a comprehensive work up and diagnostic assessment.

Through all stages of life, all persons are entitled to live their lives to the fullest within the limits of their capabilities and desires and not be brushed aside or dismissed because of age or physical infirmities. The caring woman must always seek the appropriate medical advice and assistance. Then it will be easier for their older loved one to live the remaining years with as much dignity as possible.

Chapter # 7: CARING WOMAN TIPS

1. **Do not ignore the signs of memory loss.** Get the older adult to a qualified physician as soon as possible.

2. **Please remember that persons with dementia are fearful.** They fear abandonment. They fear new situations, new people and new sounds. Think if you got off a plane in a foreign country, did not read or understand the language and

needed to find a bathroom or your hotel: You would be frustrated and frightened.

3. **Accept that dementia cannot be "fixed" or cured.** It is a degenerative disease that ends in death. Total decline can take from 5 to 20 years.

4. **Behaviors can be different with visitors:** Quite often, when family members, siblings or friends visit the older adult, their behavior may seem normal. They can rise to the occasion. When the visitors leave, it is back to the way you see them daily. This can be extremely frustrating for the caring woman, as the visiting relatives or friends tell her that the older person is "not that bad!" Perhaps you can explain to them before they visit that this person you are seeing today is not quite the same on a 24/7 basis.

5. **It's more important to be kind than be right.** People with advancing dementia live in the moment. Being truthful can cause stress for both the caring woman and the older adult. Does it really matter that the older adult thinks it is Tuesday when it is Friday? Or, believes that the person stopping by is a friend rather than a paid care provider? As a caring woman, you can offer support and comfort by "bending the truth" for your impaired adult. Because we were brought up to not lie to our parents, learning to tell "fiblets"

is often difficult, but is, frankly, more kind. With practice, it will become easier.

6. **Straightforward, simple statements, given one at a time, are usually the best way to gain cooperation.** When an older adult is saying things or acting in ways that do not make sense, our tendency is to carefully explain the situation and expect them to understand and comply. However, with dementia, there may not be rational thinking. It's also very easy to underestimate how challenging a "normal" task is now for your loved one. ***Example:*** *Saying, "it is time to brush your teeth," may bring confusion. Brushing one's teeth involves many steps: going down the hall, finding the bathroom, turning on the light, locating the right toothbrush, putting on toothpaste, turning on the water, brushing, etc. You may have to give these steps to the older parent one at a time.*

7. **Making agreements with the older adult who has dementia does not always work.** They may not be capable of remembering what you told them not to do, such as using a walker or *not* turning on the stove. For some with early dementia, leaving notes may help. For others, it won't. You cannot change them, only your reaction to them and their behaviors.

8. **On good days, it is perfectly normal to question a diagnosis of dementia.** There may be times when

rational thinking and appropriate responses occur. This is when you may think that your older adult has been misdiagnosed or the problem exaggerated. The older adult is just having one of their lucid times. Treasure them! You cannot predict when the next one may come along.

9. **It is easy to both overestimate and underestimate your parent's capabilities.** As a caring woman you may find it easier to do something for your older loved one rather than let them do it for themselves. However, if your parent can manage a task, doing it will give them a feeling of satisfaction. On the other hand, if coerced into a certain task or activity *beyond* their capabilities, then frustration and agitation may result. Finding the balance for your older loved one can be a constant struggle and can shift from day to day—from confusion to awareness, from refusal to cooperation.

10. **The caring woman cannot do it all; ask for help before you feel desperate.** When people offer to help, say "YES." Make a list of what you need done: bring a meal, pick up a prescription, trim the roses, or stay with the older adult so you can have some respite. This will reinforce offers of help. If you know you will be needing someone to assist you with the care of the older adult suffering from dementia, the earlier you introduce a care provider in the disease process

the more acceptable it will be to the older adult. This person will not be "a stranger," which can be frightening to them.

11. **Become aware of your facial expressions and tone of voice when speaking to a person with dementia; they are sensitive to your emotions.** If you are angry, sad, or frustrated, they can pick up on it and react. They can pick up on happiness, too. Never approach them from behind. It can frighten them. When they become anxious, some favorite music from their past can be soothing.

12. **It's a long, progressively worsening journey, so ask for help and give yourself the care you need to survive this process.** Regardless of the cause of your older parent's dementia, you, the caring woman, need to realize that their abilities are declining. Your parent is "unlearning" the tasks of which they were so capable a few weeks or months ago. It is not easy to watch and can be frustrating and heartbreaking. So please take care of you. Find out all you can about the disease process, ask for help and learn to give yourself hugs as you are doing a heroic job seeing to the well-being and safety of your older parent who is gradually disappearing.

Chapter 8

DRIVING: When is it time to stop?

This seems to be the universal question that caring women face when they see their older parent declining physically or having memory problems.

For most of us, driving is a symbol of status, control and independence. Getting your driver's license was a rite of passage that allowed a delicious new freedom at a time when parents and social authorities were questioning your activities and behaviors.

Understandably, after decades behind the wheel, your older parent has a sense of expertise and does not like to be questioned about their ability to drive. For older adults, even those who face health issues or increasing forgetfulness, driving may be the single most important symbol of independence, as driving allows them to have experiences they might otherwise miss.

Imagine being asked to give up any portion of control or independence regarding *your* daily routine—especially by an adult child. Your older parent's rebellious, resistant response to the threat of losing their last bastion of independence may seem similar to an adolescent's behavior. Is it any wonder then that being asked to give up driving or relinquish the car keys can be a major life event?

As a caring woman, the challenge is how to preserve the sense of freedom and mobility essential to your older parent's quality of life and well-being, without endangering themselves or others. Think about when it might be time for your parent to give up the keys. If or when the time comes for the older parent to stop driving, it will most likely impact your life. Planning ahead for this critical juncture will make the transition easier and safer for everyone.

Remember that driving is a skill that requires judgment, attention, and decision-making. Thinking about their ability with these can give you a more thoughtful approach in talking with your parent. When these skills are impaired in an older parent with memory loss or physical and/or mobility limitations, it affects their reaction time and response to danger. As a caring woman, it is vitally important to prepare for this loss. The consequences of your parent driving when they no longer have the skills versus the confrontation with your parent that you'd give anything to avoid can be disastrous, with you having to pick up the pieces.

Two Recent News Headlines:

Senior accelerates car into Saturday morning Farmer's Market. He was driving under the influence of a powerful, new to him, medication. He killed 11 people, including two toddlers.

75-year-old man with dementia missing for 3 days. He was last seen getting into his truck with his dog and driving north on Hwy 101. Two months later, the man's malnourished dog walked on to a rancher's property. Six months later, the man's truck was located on an isolated mountain road; the man has yet to be found.

The following is a story that did not make the headlines:

Diane's Story: *Diane came for a consultation with a geriatric care manager (GCM) regarding her mother's declining mental abilities. Her mother, Abigail, was living on her own in an apartment near her daughter and still driving, but "only to the store and to the beauty parlor," Diane related. Abigail came to Diane's for dinner once a week, and arriving late on several occasions, said she had turned on the wrong street.*

At other times, when Diane visited her mother, she found old food in the refrigerator, the laundry not done, houseplants drooping and dying (and these were her mother's babies). Abigail also had an odor that suggested urinary incontinence, which she denied. The more descriptions Diane gave to the GCM about her mother's behaviors and forgetfulness, the more alarming the picture became. It was the proverbial flashing red light.

In talking to Diane, the geriatric care manager felt it might be time for Abigail to move to an assisted living facility. Diane thought it was not time until her mother "got worse."

"At least go and look at some nearby facilities so you will know what suits your mother best, when the time does come," the GCM suggested. Two weeks later Diane called the GCM to say that she was moving her mother into an ALF. The previous week Abigail had been on her way

to her weekly hair appointment and apparently made a wrong turn and went missing for 24 hours, driving around trying to find her way home. Meanwhile Diane was frantic!

Relating the anguish she felt, Diane figured that her mother had driven at least 75 miles, maybe more, yet had enough rational thinking to stop for gas. Abigail returned with blisters on her hands from gripping the steering wheel so hard for so long. Diane was extremely fortunate that her mother returned safely, as too often the older parent becomes lost and is never seen again.

Yes, it can happen in a minute or less when the older adult with dementia becomes confused and disoriented.

Where to Start THE TALK

If you are concerned about your older adult's driving abilities, carefully initiate a discussion about driving, perhaps using a news article or a story about a friend's near accident. Be very gentle in your approach as their driving means their independence. If you realize the discussion is not going anywhere, then stop, but read on for more tips.

Meanwhile, find out what medications your loved one is taking and any side effects. Does your older adult have any vision or hearing deficits? These are health issues that can impair driving, along with some heart conditions, arthritis, previous strokes, and/or Parkinson's disease.

Since dementia is an organic brain disorder, it brings with it impaired cognition involving memory and judgment.

Many physicians allow their older adult patients with mild memory impairment or early stage dementia to continue driving. From what is known about dementia, the changes in the brain can happen quickly, although this varies from person to person. However, from my perspective, it is better to error on the side of caution and have your older adult stop driving before things become dire.

Older adults with moderate or severe dementia cannot respond rationally to their environment. They may be unable to remember their destination and may be inattentive to pedestrians or oncoming traffic. Judgement is slow or poor and they cannot make quick decisions when necessary. With so many cars on the road traveling at higher speeds, having all of one's faculties is a must.

As people age, their responses are not as quick and the eyes take longer to adjust from up close (the speed on the odometer) to the distance of who's ahead of you on the road. Other changes, such as eye surgery, can change depth perception and focus.

A PERSONAL STORY: *My mother had serious eye surgery that resulted in blurred vision lasting for several months. Even though she was told not to drive, she still did but "only to the beauty parlor," she insisted. However, the street she took to get there had many children playing on sidewalks and sometimes in the street.*

My concern was their safety. What if a child ran out into the street chasing a ball? Would she see him? Could she stop in time? My mother would not listen to my concerns.

Somewhere in one of our conversations, she questioned my former husband's morals.

I took this opportunity and asked, "Do you think it is morally right to drive when you cannot see well enough and were told not to by the doctor?" Oh, was she shocked that I confronted her in this manner! However, it worked. She had a neighbor take her until her eyes were completely healed.

When you know they should no longer be behind the wheel, find a way to get them to stop driving. **PLEASE.**

Often fibs (aka fiblets) are necessary as rational thinking does not work. "Since you have not driven the car for a while, I found that it would not start," is a good one. A few suggestions: disabling the car; hiding the keys; mentioning the high cost of insurance or smog testing. Finance based reasons may work best, as many of these folks, with dementia or not, are still money-conscious.

The AARP website has many good suggestions under Driver Safety (at the bottom of its opening page), including an online seminar called "We Need to Talk," with suggestions on how to have this conversation

The following are warning signs from the above website:

1. Almost crashing, with frequent "close calls."
2. Finding dents and scrapes on the car, on fences, mailboxes, garage doors, curbs, etc.

3. Getting lost, especially in familiar locations.
4. Having trouble seeing or following traffic signals, road signs and pavement markings.
5. Responding more slowly to unexpected situations or having trouble moving their foot from the gas to the brake pedal; confusing the pedals.

A PERSONAL STORY: *My Dad gave up driving when he accelerated backing out of the garage instead of braking. He hit and went over the retaining wall, severely damaging the underside of his old Lincoln aka "the Tank." My brother and I were lucky that our Dad voluntarily quit driving after this mishap.*

6. Misjudging gaps in traffic at intersections and on highway entrance and exit ramps.
7. Causing other drivers to honk or complain.
8. Easily becoming distracted or having difficulty concentrating while driving.
9. Having a hard time turning around to check the rear view while backing up or changing lanes.
10. Receiving multiple traffic tickets or "warnings" from law enforcement officers.

If you notice one or more of these cautionary signs in yourself or in an older adult who is driving, you might want to register for a driver-improvement course, such as the classroom or online courses offered by AARP.

Go to www.aarp.org for more information.

Before your discussion, review the options:

1. Maybe your parent would be willing to sign up for a driver education class with AARP if you went along with them. These classes are frequently offered at local senior centers. Or you can locate one near you on the AARP website.

2. Perhaps your parent can travel with others for shopping trips, medical visits or church services.

3. If you need to move your parent closer to you, then choose a house, an apartment or other residence that is close to shopping, services and a hospital.

4. To maintain a higher potential of health and fitness, gently suggest engaging in daily physical and mental activity.

Explore (and propose using) alternative transportation:

1. Contact your local transportation department: They may have a special service for older adults, such as low-cost taxi vouchers or Dial-a-Ride.

2. Contact your local senior center for their recommendations. Many have vans that can transport locally for a small fee.

3. See if a neighbor might be able to help with transportation.

4. Go online to your local Office on Aging to review transportation options.

5. Find and pay for someone close by to drive them to shopping and appointments.

License Renewal

Your state licensing agency may require renewal applicants to undergo physical or mental examinations or to retake the vision, written and/or road tests, if the older adult's fitness to drive is in doubt. Doubt may be created in a numbers of ways including:

- The older adult's appearance or demeanor at the renewal appointment
- A history of accidents or violations
- Reports by physicians or others
- Failing the vision test

In many states, physicians are mandated to report a patient with moderate or severe dementia to the Department of Motor Vehicles. If you are concerned about your parent's driving ability, then speak to their doctor about your concerns.

If that does not get you the results you need, then you can make an anonymous report to the DMV, stating that you think that your parent or other older adult is too impaired to drive responsibly. Then the DMV sends the older adult a letter asking them to make an appointment for a verbal and/or written test to determine their fitness to drive. If determined to be unfit, then they are issued an ID card that is very similar to a driver's license. Most DMV offices are gentle in their evaluation and usually tell the older driver that they can come in again when they are feeling better to be retested. For many, that satisfies them for the present. Although you may hear them frequently ask you when can they go back to the DMV to try again this is the opportunity for you to use a "fiblet".

CHAPTER 8: CARING WOMAN TIPS
Helpful Hints for a Successful Discussion

1. **Be sure to focus more on solutions and alternatives for assistance so they don't feel attacked when you point out their driving problems.**

2. **Changes and decisions are to be made *with* the parent, and not for the parent, if possible.**

3. **If you should reach an impasse about a necessary change, a word from the physician, clergyman**

or geriatric care manager may bring the desired result.

4. **Giving up a car does not mean the older adult needs to be stuck at home.** Emphasize that there is still mobility between public, private and hired transportation.

5. **Saving money can be an attractive incentive.** Remind the older adult that the expenses of gas, maintenance, insurance and registration fees will go away when they give up driving.

6. **When the older parent does stop driving, make sure there are plenty of visitors and opportunities for interaction with others.** Social isolation can lead to or increase depression.

7. **Emphasize your concern for the other drivers.** During your discussion, find an opportunity to say that it is not you, it is the other people on the road that I am worried about and how they are driving, which is probably too fast.

Go to the AARP website (www.aarp.com) under Driver Safety for additional information.

Chapter 9:

Mortality: the End of a Journey

Death is a mystery. How much do we really know about it? Only that it is a certainty for all living creatures and can come at any age and any time. Perhaps it is this unknown quality that makes so many fearful of its finality. Since today's culture wants quick fixes, it is left with the puzzlement of how to cope with death. For many, the end of life is accompanied by pain, loss of bodily functions and unresolved issues with family, property and life.

Yet, everyone wants a comfortable death—for their loved ones and for themselves. So how do we get there? We get there by a better understanding of what *needs* to be done and what *cannot* be done to make the end of life's journey be as peaceful as possible.

Many frail older adults would welcome death as an escape from the physical and/or mental indignities brought about by age or disease. In a hurry to finish their journey, they want it over with as quickly as possible and may talk about dying in their sleep or taking too many pills. Meanwhile, they await the relief and peace that death offers...and the unknown.

Caring women may see it differently and are often not ready for the finality of death—wanting to postpone it can be a natural reaction. The impending death of an older parent can bring up feelings of denial, anger, guilt, bargaining and, finally, acceptance, noted Elizabeth Kubler-Ross in her landmark studies of death and dying.

Denial comes when we cannot face losing the parent and think that what is happening may be an incorrect diagnosis. Anger may take the form of an adult child's lashing out at medical personnel, who cannot fix the illness, or with the parent for not wanting to get better.

Some family members may want to delay death with medications or heroic treatments in the futile hope that the older parent will recover. Unfortunately, the truth is that these actions may prolong the pain and the indignity of the older parent's final round with life.

Only in recent years have folks needed to make a choice between life and death. Medical technology has, in many cases, gone beyond ethics and common sense. Such as, a son having to make a decision for a feeding tube to prolong life without quality due to advanced dementia versus slipping away into the arms of death and dying quietly. Many so called "life-saving benefits" can cause additional pain and heartache to both the dying patient and caring family members. When death seems imminent, families frequently need to make hard choices.

The benefit of a particular treatment may not improve the quality of life—and may well increase the emotional burden to the dying person and the family. The benefit versus burden debate is an ongoing one, and does not have a winner. What one person may see as a benefit, such as the extension of life for a few weeks, may seem burdensome for the dying person who may be facing more "trial" drugs, excruciating pain and diminishing quality of life.

Ideally, the goals of medical treatment should be established at the time a diagnosis of chronic or terminal illness is made. This is when to bring as many family members together as possible to find out the physician's recommendations and what may be the benefits, side effects and probable outcomes of a particular treatment.

The three possible goals of medical treatment are:

- Cure
- Stabilization of Function
- Death with Comfort and Dignity

Sometimes goals can be combined, such as a patient with terminal cancer may choose an antibiotic treatment for pneumonia. Technologies, such as ventilators, feeding tubes, chemotherapy and radiation have improved some patient's odds of surviving but if the older adult has multiple medical problems, there may be little to gain and the outlook less than optimistic. It is important that older adults discuss their desires about the use of life-prolonging medical treatments with their families and put these wishes in writing.

Facing the death of a parent is a distressing reality that is, more times than not, avoided or denied. Each individual has their own definition of quality of life and, ideally, this will be revealed in discussion with family members. If there are differences of opinion among family members, then it is appropriate to seek the help of a physician, medical social worker, clergy or a geriatric care manager to mediate the discussion. Then, emotional and spiritual preparations for dying can occur and may even work in tandem with the treatment of symptoms that could bring death at any time.

ELLA'S STORY: *Ella was a 74-year-old woman who had been having severe abdominal pains for many months. Her doctor had prescribed numerous treatments and medications as solutions, with no relief. Upon the suggestion of a friend, Ella visited another physician who, upon examining her, immediately hospitalized her. The diagnosis was metastasized ovarian cancer.*

For years Ella had told doctors that she had a hysterectomy, which Ella understood to be complete removal of the uterus and ovaries. Not so. Ella had never married and her closest relative was Anne, a niece. When the oncologists talked with Ella and Anne, it was suggested and agreed upon that Ella would have chemotherapy. However, her heart and kidneys were at risk, so there was only one kind of chemo treatment appropriate for her condition which, she was told, might give her three or four more months of life.

The result of the first treatment was severe diarrhea. Ella decided she would rather die than suffer this humiliating side effect.

Well, the niece and doctors stood at her bedside and became angry that she would not continue the treatments.

Ella said she wanted to die and to do it peacefully. Her friends rallied to the cause and spent the next 10 days at her bedside talking, comforting and praying with her—even getting into the hospital bed to hold her when she became fearful.

One evening, Ella was sitting up in bed with a straw flower container on her head, telling every bawdy joke she knew — and they were numerous from her time as a character actress in New York and the West Coast. She was laughing and surrounded by laughter. Ella died in her sleep that night and accomplished dying her own way.

Acceptance and caring are the keys to a comfortable experience with death. Our parents' time is finite, its amount known only to the Infinite. The final days with them can be used to prepare both them and ourselves for their departure. Preparing for a loved one's death may sound morbid and uncaring. Yet, if we love and care about them, which we do, warts and all, the caring woman wants their end as peaceful and comfortable as possible.

Preparation is a must and will benefit all concerned. The immediacy of completing the practical and necessary aspects of dying needs to be emphasized. Denial at this stage is useless and detrimental.

Dealing with Practical Death Issues

The practical aspects of death comprise both minute and complex details including:

- legal matters
- financial matters
- memorial services
- burial arrangements
- disposition of personal and real property according to the older parent's wishes

For the caring woman, making and checking a list is extremely helpful. The following can be used as a guide:

IMPORTANT ARTICLES	LOCATION
Safety Deposit Key	
Bank Account Information	
Health Insurance Policy	
Social Security Card	
Medicare/Health Insurance Cards	
Life Insurance Policy	
Home or Property Deed of Sale	
Will	
Living Trust (if applicable)	
Living Will (or Medical Directive)	

Power of Attorney

Income Tax Returns

Pre-Paid Burial Plot or Vault Receipt

Funeral Instructions

Birth Certificate

Marriage License

Divorce Papers

Important Contracts

Mortgages

Credit Card Accounts

Inventory of Personal Property

To ease your workload, be sure that clear title is established on all real property and also determine what treasured memento goes to which relative. Plan and possibly pay in advance for funeral arrangements, as the emotions of grieving affect decision-making abilities. Doing these chores ahead of time, and many times they may *feel* like chores, will bring you comfort. It also gives you a chance to speak with your parent and locate necessary and often vital information to settle their estate regardless of its size. You may also need their signature on various papers. If the older loved one was in the military, look into any veteran's benefits that may be available at www.va.gov.

MY DAD'S STORY:

My dad was on Hospice the last eight months of his life. Knowing how responsible and organized my dad was, I thought he might want to have a decision in his memorial arrangements. I asked him which funeral home he preferred, then we ironed out the details.

From the experience of making the arrangements for my mother, who had died, 12 years earlier, he knew it would be costly. So his first priority was not to spend a lot as he wanted my brother and me to have the money. The funeral home and memorial park was one where many celebrities had been laid to rest, including Marilyn Monroe; my expectation was that it would be pricey.

Armed with my dad's preferences, I entered the posh reception area and was greeted by the funeral director. He brought out the book of caskets and opened to the top-of-the-line page with the fancy bronze model. When I said to the funeral director that I wanted to see the least expensive casket, the man gasped in shock. I told him that was what my dad wanted "and if you doubt me, you can call him and talk to him yourself!"

That settled the matter and we proceeded with the details...and let me tell you there were a myriad of details and expenses involved in even the cheapest version! I also worked with a friend to pick the readings, the music and write the obituary. When my beloved dad did pass, I was so relieved that I had preplanned the arrangements and the service; it definitely made my feelings of loss and sadness less stressful.

All of these issues become the caring woman's responsibility and headache, so resolving as much as possible before the parent's death is crucial. Practical preparation can save a lot of unnecessary expense and trauma as county, state and federal regulations require exact accounting. If your parent resists, suggest to them that they can lessen your workload by directing you to the documents and deeds necessary for the settlement of their estate, then gain their input and assistance to finalize the details.

Coming to the end of life often brings up many emotional and spiritual issues—and unfinished business. The dying process can deeply test your loved one's sense of self-worth and self-respect. The parent may say they feel purposeless and burdensome. The caring woman can help them find meaning at this time by sharing a memory, a smile, a joke or a kind word. A favorite film and/or their kind of music can be soothing and serve as a distraction. Admire your loved one for their accomplishments, ask them about the lessons they have learned, and how they made it through their trials and tribulations. The time of waiting for death can become a time of sharing and reviewing life's meaningful experiences and actually create pleasant memories. Look to find those good things for which they can be honored. Our parents do deserve honor for the progress they made, as the journey through life is not easy.

It is up to us, the caring women to make the dying process a time of dignity—a time of peace and harmony. Let conversations flow naturally. For many older adults their physical losses and mental challenges have made them feel helpless and fearful. An unreasonable demand on them for resolutions of past events or hurtful experiences is often futile and can create anxiety. If some issues remain unresolved, forgiving them and letting go of past hurts may be the best, most practical and kindest solution.

HOSPICE: Comfort Care for the Dying

Deciding to shift from a treatment goal to comfort care (Hospice) is often a difficult decision for the dying person and their family. Comfort care is contrary to the way many physicians are trained, and also to the mission of hospitals, which exist primarily to cure patients. The goal of Hospice is to affirm the quality of life rather than the length of life, offering respect for the physical body and dignity for the human spirit.

When the decision is made to abandon the idea of "a cure," this is the time for Hospice. They consider all aspects at the end of life, by providing physical, emotional and spiritual comfort. Hospice is not a place, but a concept of compassionate care offered by a team of professionals, care that can take place in the home, a residential care facility, or a nursing home. It recognizes that dying is a natural process and places emphasis on the management of pain and other symptoms. In order to provide the optimum care, the team interacts with the dying person, the primary caregiver, family members and paid care providers.

The psychological and social challenges that confront persons in the process of dying, are often more distressing than the illness itself. While helping the primary caregiver or paid care provider with everyday practical care, the Hospice team also offers emotional and spiritual support during this stressful time by assisting with the inevitable feelings of grief and loss.

Knowing that this kind of support is available 24/7 can bring peace of mind to everyone. By providing the dying person with as much comfort and fulfillment as possible, it creates a compassionate environment where family members and friends can say "I love you" and "good bye".

What to Expect from Hospice Care

The goal of Hospice is to keep the dying person emotionally and physically comfortable as possible by working with the patient, the primary caregiver, family members and paid care providers. Hospice consists of an individualized plan of care designed for your loved one at home or in a facility with supportive care for both the dying person and their family.

Ideally, dying persons prefer being cared for at home where they welcome the comfort of family, friends and familiar possessions. However, some families find their skills are inadequate to cope with the many aspects of caregiving, such as special treatments, physical care, incontinence, emotional conditions, a feeling of confinement, or fear of dying and death.

Many times the care required can be overwhelming, especially in cases of dementia. Since most Hospice situations require 24/7 care, it may necessitate hiring a paid care provider or placement in an appropriate facility, to alleviate the physical and emotional stress on the primary care provider. If you chose a care facility be sure that it has a Hospice waiver, which means that the care providers have been trained in Hospice care.

Hospice should be called sooner rather than later as it offers the dying person and their family so much in the way of physical and emotional support. Anyone can refer to Hospice, however, the primary physician must certify that the dying person has a life expectancy of six months or less. If the dying person lives beyond the six month period, and qualifies, then the Hospice nurse can re-certify them. Hospice care can also be stopped at any time due to improvement in health or a change in circumstances.

Marybeth's Story

Marybeth's dad, Fred, had been on Hospice for several months. During that time Fred had moved from his home to his daughter's, as his wife could no longer care for him due to her own health challenges. The Hospice team was as caring as Marybeth and, in small ways, Fred's condition seemed to improve.

The music therapist made a weekly visit. On one of these days, while Fred and Marybeth were sitting and enjoying the music, Fred was inspired to get up and dance...and dance he did! The next day the Hospice nurse called and said that they were taking Fred off Hospice as his health seemed vastly improved. It stayed that way for another 18 months, when he again qualified for Hospice care.

This story demonstrates that Hospice care can be flexible, since it really is based on the needs of the patient.

The Hospice team usually consists of a doctor, nurse, social worker, home health aide, a spiritual chaplain and a volunteer visitor. Hospice personnel are carefully screened and trained to relate empathetically to the dying person and to offer genuine warmth and affection. Other specialists such as physical, occupational and/or musical therapists may be called in as needed or desired. The Hospice nurse most often acts as the team leader by coordinating the dying person's plan of care with the primary physician, and then monitoring and supervising the plan. The team usually meets off-site biweekly to assess and reevaluate the plan of care.

Hospice considers the "unit" of care to be the dying person *and* their family, whomever that may include: a spouse, relatives, a life partner and close friends. One of these is considered the primary caregiver, who then becomes an important member of the Hospice team. The primary caregiver plays a vital role in keeping the team up-to-date on the dying person. The Hospice team provides emotional and physical support to the primary caregiver as well as teaching how to give basic care. They can teach the caregiver about the dying process and what may be expected. The routine day-to-day care continues to be the responsibility of the family caregiver, who is also responsible to notify the Hospice team leader of any changes in the dying individual's condition. After the death, Hospice also offers grief counseling to family members, if desired.

Ninety percent of Hospice patients have a diagnosis of cancer, advanced dementia, end-stage cardiovascular disease, end-stage renal failure, HIV-related conditions or debility (often referred to as failure to thrive or multi system organ failure). Most people are uncomfortable with the idea of stopping the all-out effort to beat the disease. Some dying persons and their families have difficulty facing death and stay in denial until death is almost imminent. Yet, postponement of death with heroics or denial of the inevitable makes the end of life more difficult for all involved.

Hospice exists to provide support and caring to persons who are in the final phase of life and enables them to preserve their human dignity and enrich the time remaining. The role of Hospice is to offer support in ways that are appropriate to the person's particular lifestyle. Hospice is available to all and its costs are reimbursable under Medicare, Medicaid, private insurance, private payments and/or other financial arrangements. Service is provided regardless of the ability to pay.

To locate a Hospice program in your area, talk with the primary physician, the hospital discharge planner or social worker, the state or local health department or the state Hospice organization. You can also call the Hospice Help Line at 1(800) 658-8898 or visit their website at www.nhpco.org.

Thinking About Your Preferences for Medical Treatment *from the Center on Health Care Ethics*:

Here are some statements for you that have been helpful for others. You may want to encourage your dying loved one to adopt or adapt one or more of these to help them express their end-of-life priorities.

- In cases of doubt, err on the side of life.
- I want those treatments that offer reasonable hope to restore me to a condition that my loved ones think I would find acceptable.
- I do not want treatment that might postpone death but probably would not restore me to a quality of life that I find acceptable.
- I do/do not want a treatment if there is some small, remote chance that it might help me.
- I want treatment decisions made with a view of my overall condition and the treatment's ability to improve it.
- I want sufficient pain medication to keep me free of pain even if the dosage necessary might shorten my life.
- I want my loved ones/professionals to make decisions about my care the way they think I would make them, if I were able.

- If I lose consciousness with no reasonable hope of ever regaining it, I want all treatment stopped (including food and fluids).
- I want the cost of treatment and its financial impact on my family/community to be considered in making decisions.

CHAPTER 9: CARING WOMAN TIPS
Allowing the End of Life to Run Smoothly

1. **Respect and honor your loved one's wishes about how they want to die.**
2. **Have a family meeting with the older adult and all of the relatives involved in the care so you are all on the same page.**
3. **Have the Advance Directive documents pertaining to the end-of-life complete and easily accessible.** That includes:
   a. **A Living Will,** which says how the person wants to be treated if unable to make their own decisions.
   b. **A Health Care Proxy,** which authorizes one or more people to communicate the older adult's wishes regarding end-of-life treatment.
   c. **A Health Care Power of Attorney**, which authorizes an individual to communicate the

older adult's medical instructions, hire and fire medical providers, access and provide the older adult's medical history, and consent to a "Do Not Resuscitate" (DNR) order. (In some cases different states require different forms.)

4. **Locate any documents that pertain to funeral or burial arrangements.** If there are none then make the appropriate arrangements prior to the older adult's death. Too often funeral homes make expensive suggestions when you are most vulnerable. If your loved one was in the military, they may qualify for Veteran's Death Benefits.

5. **Waiting for an older loved one to die can be sad, stressful and heart-wrenching.** It is suggested that you get as much of the post death needs done prior to their death as possible as there is much paperwork to be finalized afterwards. Loss and grief can affect decision making. In order for things to get done and out of the way quickly, you may make emotional decisions in haste and regret them later.

6. **Seek out and use Hospice services sooner than later.** Hospice services can be stopped at any time or possibly renewed after six months. Also, Hospice helps reduce the costs involved in terminal illness and the process of dying.

Hospice services offer emotional and spiritual support, thereby enabling the dying individual and family to achieve and maintain their optimal level of functionality. Hospice is a benefit to all involved.

Chapter 10:

MEN AS CAREGIVERS: It's Just Different.

For decades the family caregiving role has fallen primarily on women, however that is changing. Unlike the common cultural perception, more men are becoming caregivers as longevity increases. Today close to one-third of primary caregivers are men according to the Alzheimer's Association and the National Multiple Sclerosis Society. The majority of these men are caring for an older parent with dementia and/or a chronic illness while others are caring for a spouse/partner with a debilitating disease such as MS, Parkinson's, or diabetes.

A man's approach to caregiving role seems to be different. It is a role for which, in many instances, they are unprepared. The majority of men have not been responsible for the ordinary household tasks of cooking, cleaning, laundry or shopping, let alone the many caregiving tasks that may involve the highly personal care of dressing, bathing or toileting, along with medication management and possible financial support. These men have to learn a great deal in a short period of time and many have difficulty coping.

Often men approach the caregiving role like their job: a work project to be managed, a problem to be solved. They may look to the Internet and/or technology for practical solutions, but neglect their relationships and – like many women, themselves. This can mean that they overlook the emotional needs of their loved ones. Even though the practical needs are taken care of, the older parent may still feel isolated and lonely without meaningful conversation or interaction.

As our society knows, men are far more reluctant to talk about their feelings, thus they may not let it be known that they are facing emotional issues in their care of an older adult. Since men as the family caregiver is a recent phenomenon, it is not talked about or discussed man-to-man or in the workplace. They are also less likely to discuss issues and concerns with family members or to seek advice or counsel in personal matters.

Even though men may hire paid caregivers, look to technology for information or available services, seeking emotional support is unusual. As a result, although men may fall prey less often to caregiver burnout, they are more prone to depression, which can lead to excess drinking, and eating or sleep deprivation.

In the his bestselling book, ***Men are from Mars; Women are from Venus***, John Gray, PhD, states that men want to fix things where women want someone to listen. This tends to be the case for men when it comes to attending a support group, calling the Alzheimer's Association or seeking resources and information from the appropriate disease organization. Men tend to think they can handle the situation without input from experienced professionals similar to the now classic not asking directions to a particular destination.

Michael's Story: *Many times over the course of a year, Michael called the facilitator of the local Alzheimer's support group to discuss his wife's "dementia" symptoms always stating that he would be at the next meeting. He never came, yet, he wanted answers. His denial was so strong about his wife's condition that he had not yet taken Susan, who was 15 years younger, for a formal diagnosis. Michael only wanted to know what he could do to make her better as her behavior was contrary to her usual personality, and she fought him on all suggestions.*

One day he showed up early at the support group and spoke with the facilitator, telling her about the diets, the natural remedies, and some of the activities he had used in an attempt to help Susan. After listening to his story, the facilitator told him, "I'm sorry, but you cannot fix it." Michael stayed that day and listened to others, all women, talk about their particular situations. When Michael's told his story to the group, one of the long time attendees told him said sadly, "I'm sorry, but you cannot fix it."

Michael obviously loved his wife and was determined that he could make her better with his strong faith, lots of prayer, the right treatment, diet or natural remedy.. He did not want to hear that by correcting Susan and arguing over small stuff with her that he was causing her to be frustrated and anxious, which lead to more stress and aggravation for her and was causing her to act out by yelling and trying to hit him.

The group encouraged him to try ignoring her mistakes and sometimes tell her "fiblets," those little white lies that are ultimately kindnesses, however he said he had never lied to her. A group participant asked Michael what difference does it make whether it is Tuesday or Thursday or if you went to the market yesterday or not at all? His wife's forgetfulness was different; it was not her, but rather the disease.

By ignoring what he could do to make his caregiving journey easier, Michael was making it harder on himself and his wife. He seemed determined to "fix" Susan's situation and it was simply not possible! He was highly stressed over their current life and, as caregivers learn, sometimes slowly, stress only exacerbates the behaviors, making it more difficult for both the loved one and the caregiver.

Sadly, Michael never returned to the group. His denial was too strong.

Sometimes with small changes, such as learning to tell *fiblets*, there is less frustration. Making the caregiving journey easier needs to become a priority or the caregiver will become the victim and possibly fall ill or die before their loved one.

Not wanting to generalize all men, there are caregiving situations taken on by men who do it well, although there usually seems to be some emotional distance when they are talking about it. Perhaps they see themselves as weak if they talk about their feelings of inadequacy or guilt. Men who are proactive can make the caregiving journey run more smoothly. By being pro-active and looking for ways to manage behaviors, resources to help and services that can be utilized, the job of caregiving can be smoother and less stressful.

> ***Mr. G's Story:*** *Mr. G lived out-of-state from his father, his remaining parent. With a suggestion from his work Employee Assistance Program, he called a geriatric care manager (GCM) near where his father lived asking for advice and assistance. After several calls and much discussion Mr. G told the GCM that he could not handle his father's care personally, as growing up, his father had been a raging, nasty alcoholic and even now would rage at him for not visiting.*
>
> *Mr. G said he would not come in person since he knew it would take him back to those awful times remembering the abuse and violence of his youth. By hiring and paying for someone else to oversee his father's care, he was being a responsible son while maintaining reasonable boundaries to protect himself from the emotional stress that so often accompanies the care of a parent.*

Oh, Brother! Here Comes the White Knight!

Frequently a mother may view her son as the better sibling just by the virtue that he is male. Even though the son makes only brief visits or calls once a week, he is seen as the White Knight, while the caregiving daughter is doing all the chores and putting up with criticism.

This scenario is not unusual. This avoidance behavior is a form of denial. Although the son does not want any part of the hands-on details of caregiving, he might offer or be asked to handle the practical chores such as household repairs if he is local or give financial assistance to hire a cleaning service or gardener if he is not. To ease resentment, the good daughter needs to ask her brother for help and be specific about what she needs done. Past that, there is little recourse but to put up with the situation or speak with her mother, explaining that it hurts her feelings that the mother is criticizing her and that she really is doing her best.

> ***A Big Brother Story:*** *Amy was the primary caregiver for her mother Louise, who lived in her own home but needed help with shopping, housecleaning, laundry and getting to doctor appointments. Louise could still bathe and dress independently. However, she would frequently forget to take her medications for high blood pressure and diabetes. Harold, the White Knight brother, stopped in briefly once or twice a week to say hello and bring his mother a flower or a cup of coffee from her favorite shop down the street.*
>
> *When Amy arrived, her mother would tell her all about Harold's visit and enthused wasn't he just a wonderful, loving son? Meanwhile, Amy gritted her teeth and put up with the constant barrage of chores and fault-finding. With the help of a support group, Amy began telling her mother that if she continued to criticize her, she would leave and not be back until the next day. After several times of saying this her mother's behavior improved. The*

group also suggested that Amy move Louise to an assisted living facility. "No, no!" Amy had exclaimed. "My mother would never go for that!"

Over the course of the following year, Louise's health deteriorated and she needed even more help with bathing, dressing and toileting. She was now also having difficulty walking and maintaining her balance. Following a really bad fall, Louise was taken to the hospital's emergency room. At the doctor's suggestion, when her mother was released from the hospital, Amy moved her mother to a very pleasant assisted living facility for physical therapy. There Louise thrived and the staff thought she was quite charming. Gone were most of the critical jibes to be replaced with a smile and a cooperative personality. Amy decided at that point to have Louise remain there. Harold now helped by supplementing the cost of the ALF and, of course, continued his brief visits...and, also, remained the White Knight!

Family dynamics and parental interaction with adult children varies from family to family. The above situation is not uncommon and most likely will continue. However, there are small changes that can be made, such as asking for practical help from the brother with the caring daughter becoming more assertive with her mother about knocking it off with the criticism and show the daughter some consideration for all her kind and attentive care.

The Good Daughter and the Supportive Spouse

Caregiving to a declining older parent is not an easy task for anyone...male or female. If the good daughter is the primary caregiver and married, her spouse can offer support by just listening. He may make constructive suggestions to improve the parent's care, or help problem solve, however criticizing is not allowed.

Caregiving is one difficult job, probably one of the most difficult jobs anyone can have in a lifetime. The caring daughter is responsible for the well-being of another adult, one who has been independent for years, and who is becoming increasingly dependent on her for *everything*. So having a mate be supportive during this caregiving journey will earn that mate zillions of brownie points!

The Creative Husband

Since men may be viewed as helpless when it comes to caregiving, they frequently receive unwanted advice from relatives and friends. Even some physicians and other health professionals who may be unfamiliar with the various behaviors that accompany dementia can frustrate the patient *and* the caregiver.

> ***Steve, the Creative Husband:*** *Steve's wife Marlene was 58 and had suffered a severe heart attack that left her with memory loss and resistant, combative behaviors. Marlene was often found sitting in the car, asking over and over to drive. Another time Steve found Marlene sitting on her horse, bareback.*

Steve was working from home in an attempt to keep Marlene with him for as long as possible. Marlene's sister, Eloise, called at least twice a week to ask how they were doing...giving heaps of advice on how Steve could better manage Marlene and the situation. After many months of this, Steve decided to call Eloise and ask if she could watch Marlene for a couple of hours as he had several business appointments.

Well, surprisingly, the appointments lasted all day from 10am to 5pm. By the time Steve picked Marlene up, Eloise had realized how much her sister's memory had failed and how difficult it was to get anything done. After that, of course, there was no more unwanted advice from her when she called Steve.

Sometime later Marlene had a hacking cough that lasted for several weeks. Steve called the doctor's office for an appointment and was told the next available one was in two weeks. "No way!" Steve thought. That day he took her to the doctor's office and waited and waited. Of course, Marlene began to act out and was disruptive to the others in the waiting room. The doctor saw her within the hour.

Sometimes caregivers need to be creative and assertive to get the job done. Bravo for Steve!

This chapter addresses those men who do not ask for help and attempt to carry the entire burden by themselves. The most adept caregivers are those who look for information and do ask for help. Some men learned this by being a single parent with young children or taking care of siblings while growing up. These men found out that by searching and looking for answers both they and their older loved ones become better for the quest.

Perhaps as more men take on the role and more studies are done to prove to them that there may be easier, better ways to handle their caregiving journey, men will be willing to listen to those with the experience or expertise that can make their caregiving journey less stressful.

Chapter 10 Tips for Caregiving Men

1. **Educate yourself.** Call the disease association associated with your loved one's medical condition to learn all you can. Find out prognoses and current treatments.

2. **Search out the resources.** Some will be available locally and/or from private agencies, such as adult day care, home care agencies and support groups.

3. **Involve family and friends.** Ask siblings for assistance and be specific about what you and your older loved one need. Accept their offers of help. Pride does not cut it in this situation.

4. **Do not try to do everything yourself.** You can't; it is impossible. You will only stress yourself out and will likely become seriously ill...or possibly die before your loved one.

5. **Join a Support Group.** It is important to talk to other caregivers who have similar challenges. This kind of support goes a long way in maintaining your sanity and in lowering your stress level.

6. **Make your own health a priority.** Look for warning signs such as sleeplessness, too much alcohol and growing feelings of discouragement and sadness. Get professional counseling if necessary. It is not a sign of weakness to ask for help; it is a sign of strength.

7. **Take respite.** Get away from caregiving for a few hours a couple of times a week, or even for a day or two. Ask friends or family to relieve you. Many assisted living facilities have rooms that can be rented for a week or two. That way, you'll know your loved one will be safe and well fed.

Chapter 11:

Decision Making 101: Making the Difficult Choice

As the caring woman you may have concerns about your older loved one's ability to remain independent. Although you might be helping out for now by dropping in to check on medications, take them shopping or to doctors' appointments they still seem to be able to manage their daily routine. What if this scenario changes and your parent or loved one has a health crisis that limits their physical capacity? What if the increasing signs of dementia become a safety concern? These changes can happen suddenly or many months from now, but they can happen. How are you going to manage the care then?

Thinking about the "what-ifs" and discussing other arrangements for care in the future is one of those not-so-pleasant issues often put off until the older adult's situation worsens. Yet, the best time to explore other choices is *now* so you can make the appropriate decision swiftly when it becomes a necessity.

If feasible, discuss future alternative living arrangements with the older adult to learn their preferences. This will give them some sense of control. When the change becomes an absolute necessity, it will be a major turning point in what remains of their life and your caregiving journey.

Understanding that there are only three ways that an older adult can be cared for in the community may be the best place to start:

1. The older adult can remain in their home with 24/7 daily personal assistance from a family member or paid care provider.

2. The older adult can move in with you and your family or another family member.

3. The older adult can move to an alternative living arrangement.

Each of these choices has its pros and cons. And each choice will find both you and the older adult somewhat dissatisfied because, chances are, making a decision like this is not what either of you wanted. None of the above situations will be perfect as the older adult's life has changed, and their life as they remember it will never be the same again.

The older adult wanted to be able to live independently until they died peacefully in their sleep. And you did not want to see them grow frail, disabled and losing control of their physical and/or mental abilities. Right now you need to focus on deciding which choice is best based on their current physical and mental capabilities.

A Realistic Look at the Options

As much as you may love the older adult, caring for them 24/7 can overwhelm even the most capable person. These loved ones are in physical decline or suffering from some form of dementia. Even though there will be times when their health problems seem to improve or level out, they will not return to their previous state of health or independence. So you will need to think this decision through clearly by keeping an open mind and obtaining realistic feedback from those who understand your unique caregiving situation.

Search out people who can assist you in clarifying the issues and be open minded with their opinions, such as friends, geriatric professionals or a support group. Be cautious about seeking the advice from close relatives or siblings, as often they cannot or will not see how the older adult has declined and how difficult the daily care has become. The latter is called denial.

Even though the choice may seem obvious, the decision to move forward with it will not be easy. You probably never thought you would have to make these decisions for your older loved one. And, you never imagined it could be so agonizing. Trying to decide on what is best for someone else is difficult enough, however, when it is an older parent or a spouse who is not feeling well and whose health is in decline, it can be monumental.

You may be thinking of what they would want, their likes and dislikes, what they are accustomed to in their present living situation, and how the older adult will react to the changes that are going to take place. Other thoughts may be: which choice is best for their care...who should care for them...which caring environment is best for their health, safety and well-being?

At this point you may feel so overwhelmed that you want to give up and accept the first solution that comes along. These feelings are normal for the circumstances.

Explore all of the possibilities and the resources that fit the personal needs and limitations of the older adult. It may ease hard feelings if the older adult understands that their safety and well-being is of utmost importance to you and thus is willing to discuss their preferences in a reasonable manner.

However, if that is *not* the case and you are frustrated and exhausted, then this is the time to seek the help and expertise of a professional: the primary physician, a geriatric care manager, or a medical social worker. When you have made the decision and know that some family members may fight you on this then ask a GCM or social worker to mediate a family meeting. Regularly attending a support group can also help as any one of them may have faced the same dilemma. By moving forward in this manner, you will find comfort in knowing that you did your best when the decision is made.

A: Staying In Their Home

More times than not the older adult will tell you that they want to stay at home until the day they die. The older loved one, as long as they are not a danger to themselves or others, is entitled to make their own decisions and their own choices. If they want to stay in their home, then you can assist them in locating the resources and services to help them remain there as long as they are appropriate.

The home will need to be made as safe as possible. Consider installing safety bars and ramps, obtaining a walker, a wheelchair, and/or a hospital bed along with additional aids for dressing, bathing and household tasks. Check with Medicare, as they pay for some of these medical aids. If not then contact your local senior center, your faith community or inquire of friends who may have these needed items. Also consider a personal emergency alarm, one that can be worn around the older adult's neck or wrist.

Many times an older adult thinks that remaining in the home is staying independent, however they do not seem to realize the amount of time and effort required to keep them there safely. Sometimes the amount of physical and emotional energy or financial resources necessitated by in-home living can be unbelievable. The physical aspects alone can burn out even the most well-intentioned and loving family caregiver. Often the wisest decision is to hire an in-home care provider, so the primary caregiver can offer the older loved one the much-needed social and emotional support.

If hesitant about hiring in-home care, ask yourself these questions:

1. *Does your older adult need more help than you can provide?*

2. *Have you given up your activities and personal time on behalf of taking care of them?*

3. *Is the time you are spending in assisting your older adult affecting your family or your job?*

4. *Do you feel exhausted or discouraged?*

If you answer "yes" to *any* one of these, then it is time you hire an in-home care provider, someone other than you who can provide for the older adult's care needs.

The thought of hiring someone to help may seem like adding more work to your already busy schedule, and you might not know where to begin. The first thing to decide is: do you want to hire through a home care agency, or do a private hire? Many families find the latter more affordable.

Although hiring through an agency may be more expensive, it is often the more practical choice, as it eliminates much of the tedious paperwork involved with a private hire. It also provides the added advantage of finding an immediate replacement should there be a personality conflict with the older adult, a no-show for work, or if the worker quits without notice. If you hire privately rather than through an agency, you may be required to provide health insurance, workman's compensation, and pay employment taxes.

Whether hiring through an agency or privately, an important first step is to determine what kind of assistance the older adult needs. Prepare a list of duties for the in-home care provider. In other words, write a job description.

Some typical duties might include supervision with the activities of daily living that the older adult is still able to do independently. Be specific about cooking, cleaning, laundry and companionship. Although the older adult may perform some of the personal care activities at a slower pace, it is important that the care provider understand that this helps to give a feeling of control over their situation.

If you hire through an agency, you are the customer and entitled to interview any potential provider. Tell them about the older adult's condition: their physical and mental capabilities and limitations. An in-home provider must know about the older adult's food preferences and its preparation, sleeping habits and any incontinence. Observe the applicants' response to this information. Ask how they would handle specific situations or emergencies. *Do not hide problems* as the applicant will not stay if the caregiving situation is not clearly presented.

The primary caregiver should not be surprised if the older adult claims that the in-home provider does not do things the way they like them done. Such a reaction is more the norm than the exception. That is the reason why it is so important to find a care provider with a compatible personality. Many older adults have long-standing, unchangeable biases or a hearing impairment that makes it difficult for them to understand a person with a strong accent.

Obtain referrals to home care agencies or private hire caregivers from reliable sources such as the support group, Alzheimer's Association, geriatric care manager, or friends who have been caregivers. *Do not* under any circumstances *advertise* in the classified ads or online as too many suspicious people are looking for a home to live in or an easy mark.

Although there are numerous details involved in hiring a home care provider, it will be well worth the effort. However, after several months or even years, the assistance the older adult needs can go beyond what you or paid caregiver can provide. Then it is time to consider an alternative living arrangement.

B: Moving In With An Adult Child

You may be making daily visits to the older adult's home, supervising medications, bringing prepared meals and assisting with the household chores. As you leave, you reassure your parent and yourself that everything will be okay. Then on the way home, you might begin worrying about their safety. If the older adult lives any distance away, the stress only increases.

Your instinctive response, as you watch your older adult struggle with chronic illness and dependency, is to offer to have them come live with you. Although this feels like a generous idea, it is not always the best option. In many cases, it can be a huge mistake. Having an older adult move in with you is a serious commitment, and you need to think long and hard before making such an offer. Good intentions do not always guarantee good results.

When contemplating this kind of long-term closeness, you will need to think about the following questions:

1. What was it like when you were younger and lived with the older adult?

2. How well do you get along with the older adult now?

3. Are there personality conflicts?

4. Was your father authoritarian? Was your mother passive and dependent or demanding of your time and attention?

Personalities do not change. You and the older adult become more of who you are as you age.

More questions:

1. How does the rest of your family feel about this?

2. Can your primary relationship withstand a significant reduction in quality time?

3. If any of your children, teenagers or young adults live with you, are any of them willing to contribute their time and effort in assisting with the older adult's care?

If strong consideration is being given to this option, call a family meeting. Be open in discussing all of the issues, as a group and as individuals. Your first responsibility is to your spouse and your children. If you and your immediate family do not come first, then resentment will arise on all sides.

Now ask yourself these questions:

1. The older adult may have felt lonely and isolated in their previous surroundings. How much attention do they expect?

2. Will they want to be entertained?

3. What are the older adult's personal care capabilities?

4. Will you be comfortable leaving them alone?

5. Will you be able to provide the care necessary for the present *and* as they become increasingly dependent? There may come a time when you will not be able to bathe or toilet the older adult. Are you able to afford the $20 to $30 per hour to hire a care provider, *and* will the older adult accept an outsider?

When an older adult who is frail and nearing the end of life moves into your home, there may be good intentions of filial warmth and sharing. Yet whether this move is by choice or default, the stage is also set for trouble unless guidelines and routines are agreed upon in advance.

By taking in your older adult, you are about to give up your privacy - and not just to anyone - but to someone who matters a great deal to you. If this older adult is your parent, then they will know all the right buttons to push to get your attention, possibly setting off feelings of resentment, anger and guilt. A look, a comment, or even a sigh can be the trigger. These feelings may be from the long ago past, feelings that you thought were gone forever. If this happens frequently, then join a support group to vent your feelings as well as gather helpful hints to assist you with this kind of living arrangement.

Why A Support Group? Response From Attendees:

It is my lifeline. By attending the group, I know that I am not alone and that others are going through similar things. I learn something new each time; sometimes about the disease and other times it is tips or strategies in dealing with the daily caregiver trials. GW

Wow, I certainly learned a lot today. Thank you all for sharing your challenges and your wins. It will help me get through the week. HS

Coming regularly to this group keeps me mentally healthy. AG

You will need to establish guidelines (boundaries) to help ease this transition. The following will help you to shape them:

Remember: You Have Your Limits

These limits mean that you will not be able to care for you older adult in the same way they cared for you. They are now an adult and so are you. Changing a diaper on a fully developed adult is not the same as changing one on an infant or a young child. If this older adult cared for their parent in past years, they may be expecting the same kind of care. It is not the same and cannot be the same.

Times Are Different For You And Them

You may have a career or a fulfilling volunteer job that you do not want to give up. Many of these older adults' lives were their home and family. Today's older adults are living longer with more chronic illnesses than ever before. Quite often, emotional ties can be barriers to care, as the roles appear to have reversed and it seems as though you are parenting your parent. Even though this is not a reality, it may seem that way to the older adult. They are losing their independence and need others to help them maintain their daily routines. That may bring up feelings of frustration or sadness...or both.

Who Is The Head Of Your Household?

The older adult may have been the boss in their home, but you and/or your spouse are in charge of yours. There may be time when the older adult does not want to cooperate or becomes rebellious. This is the time to be assertive. If the older adult interferes with your role as spouse or parent, you will need to put a stop to it immediately. Some older adults have been known to create a disruptive triangle in a long-term marriage. Be aware of these emotional minefields.

A Brief Story of Manipulation:

Lois brought her 92-year old physically frail mother, Edna, to live with her and her husband. This was out of financial necessity. In the past, Edna always had the attention and companionship of men and had always known how to manipulate them. After several months Lois began to notice that her husband, Roy, quite often took the mother's side and was becoming critical of the way things were done in the home and the care being given.

After attending a support group, Lois spoke to her husband privately about the situation and, although hesitant at first, he did come to understand the problems Edna was creating. They talked to Edna together and gave her the choice of changing her behavior or moving to a nursing home. Of course, there was denial, but gradually Edna softened and gentle reminders helped. Giving an ultimatum may seem like a hard line to take, but the marriage comes ***first.***

Outline Your Daily Routine, Make Guidelines and Assign Tasks

You will need to make a list of your daily/weekly household routine. This will clarify your responsibilities to yourself and your family. Do not allow yourself to become the maid or the servant. Give your older adult a chore (s), keeping in mind their present limitations, even if it's only putting away the silverware or folding the laundry. In this way, they can feel useful. Be very specific about the sharing of expenses, (telephone and utility bills, groceries), noise levels, smoking, and entertaining guests. When the older adult moves in with you, they become part of the family, not a guest.

Protect Everyone's Privacy

You will need to make sure that everyone has some privacy; that is a space where you, your spouse or your parent can be alone. It is okay to make some rooms off-limits. If your parent wants to entertain guests, then they need to let you know when, where and how. You will need to be very clear on all of these things as well as about going out to dinner and on vacations. Do they come with the family or do they stay home with a paid care provider?

Your older adult may enjoy attending an adult day center, which offers structured activities and gives you time off for your personal needs.

Personal Endorsements From Adult Day Center Users

"I was able to leave my mother at the Adult Day Center, go to work and not worry about her safety and well-being and she too, had a good day!! The woman I picked up in the afternoon was not the same quiet person I dropped off in the morning. She was talkative, laughing, quick to respond and her sense of humor was definitely there. For a little while each day I had my mom back." SLB

"My mother was tired and bored spending her days only seeing and talking to me. At the Adult Day Center she had

new faces and this stimulated her. She talked more, was happier and began sleeping better." RLS

"The Adult Day Center aka 'The Club' was an absolute godsend to me and my family!" HDT

"Dad had other men to talk with and tell the same stories over and over again. The staff is so kind and patient." DGF

Pick Your Battles

When the tension rises (and it will), you will have to decide what you can live with and what you cannot. Everyone in the family will need to make compromises. If the television volume is an irritation, then purchase earphones for the older adult. Also having a separate phone, perhaps a simple flip phone for the older adult, will give them more independence.

Establish a forum for complaints. Big or small problems will need to be brought up before they can fester and become troublesome. You will need to decide ahead of time how complaints will be handled, giving all family members a chance to express themselves. Let everyone offer solutions, no matter how absurd they may sound.

Give It Time

At first you may have to endure some rough spots. Changes in life always take adjustment, especially for an older adult who has given up their home and independence. This new living arrangement and the smoothing out process will take time. You will need to be patient, kind and firm before making any decisions that may change the present arrangement. This time can be enriching for the family, too, as it can give grandchildren and other relatives a chance for reminiscing.

Know When To Quit

If after giving this living arrangement a reasonable amount of time, (the time-frame is up to you), the situation has not settled down, or the older adult's care has progressed beyond your capabilities and you are stressed out, reconsider this decision. A good place to start is to listen to your body, your mind and your heart. Is your health being affected? Are you and your spouse having more arguments and spending less time together? Are the younger family members behaving poorly and staying in their rooms more than usual?

Listen to your instincts and realize that this arrangement may not be working out. It is better to make a change before you are emotionally drained and physically exhausted. Look into alternative living arrangements before you discuss this with the older adult. You will need to talk to the older adult about any changes so they can prepare for it. The transition from moving to your home to another living environment will be smoother if it is done before resentment and anger builds to the boiling point.

This time of life is not easy for the older adult or for you. Neither one of you expected this to happen: their dependency, their frailty, and needing assistance to manage a daily routine, was not how either of you pictured your loved one's older years. Nonetheless, your spouse, your marriage, your children and your job need a complete and whole person, not one who is fragmented and strained to the point of collapse.

Yes, it happens all the time; it's called Caregiver Burnout. Don't let it happen to you.

Open your mind and your heart to change and to other alternatives and choices. In the long run, it is better for all.

C: Moving To An Alternative Living Environment

The decision to place an older loved one in alternative living arrangement is probably one of the hardest decisions any caregiver can face. That is the reason it is important to become familiar with the various housing alternatives available. Remember the saying "home is where the heart is?" This applies to the independence older adults associate with their personal domain, their home. Almost all have great difficulty making the decision to leave their home, with all its memories and pleasant times; they did not want to move to "one of *those* places."

There may come an occasion when you might have to make this decision for them. If their physical body is declining to the point where they are falling frequently or perhaps calling you twenty or more times a day due to their increasing dementia, then it is time. Maybe, they left the gas on, burned their food, or left the water run to overflowing. Again, it is time. In addition the home may no longer be safe for them due to deferred maintenance. ***Their safety comes first.***

Having the older adult move out of their home into an alternative living environment for their safety is a loving act. You will need to reassure them, over and over again in different ways, that you are not abandoning them. You can tell them that this housing situation is able to provide the services they need that will allow them the time and freedom to pursue hobbies, make new friends and participate in various planned social activities. If they continue to ask when will they go back home, then reassure them with a small *fiblet*: "You can return home when a doctor says you're strong enough".

The Unhappy Older Parent:

As was mentioned in Chapter 2, you cannot make your older loved one happy if they have never been happy. Noreen's mother, Josie, came to live with her. After several months, Noreen realized that Josie's physical needs were more than Noreen could handle and still keep working. In addition, Josie was constantly complaining about everything...the weather, missing her home, the care she was receiving, the way the food was prepared. On and on it went!

Noreen talked with her sister, Marianne, and they decided it was better if Josie moved to an Assisted Living Facility (ALF). Noreen found a lovely ALF in her town. At first Josie thought it was great, then after a month or so, the complaints began; the same ones that Noreen had experienced plus criticisms of the other residents. Her mother was unhappy and felt there was a better place. The sisters agreed that a better place was the answer.

Marianne looked into the ALFs in her area, about 100 miles away, and located a lovely home that the sisters thought even they could live in. Josie moved and again, after a few months the complaints began. Now the sisters were once more looking for a new place where their mother would be happy. It doesn't exist. It was suggested to the sisters, that since Josie was mentally capable, she could call and search for a better place herself. After a number of phone calls, Josie gave up. With the help of a support group, Noreen and Marianne learned to diffuse or ignore the complaints. They frequently had to remind themselves that you cannot make a lifelong complainer stop complaining.

One of the most tedious decisions faced by the caring daughter is choosing an alternative living arrangement suitable to the needs of an increasingly dependent older loved one. The amount of dependency will affect your choice of the level of care required. Too often older adults and caring daughters wait until there is a crisis before they even begin to think about an alternative living arrangement. Then they might make a hasty choice that is regretted later. *Planning ahead for all possibilities makes the decision of when and where to move run more smoothly.*

Visit at least three appropriate housing locations, seeking the one most suitable. Again, if possible, discuss all aspects of the move with the older adult and other family members. Since there are positive and negatives in any move, make a list of the pros and cons, then rest on it, but only briefly.

For the older adult's protection and safety, the decision to move needs to made as soon as possible.

Descriptions of Alternative Living Arrangements

The following living options represent different "levels of care." There are distinctions in each.

Senior Apartments

These are individual apartments for the independent older adult. They should be equipped with bathroom safety features, emergency pull cords, locked entry doors, and a receptionist who keeps tabs on the older adult's whereabouts. These units offer security, laundry facilities, and a limited number of parking spaces for those older adults who are still driving. They are usually located near shopping and transportation. Some apartment complexes may offer scheduled transportation and/or a daily communal meal for an additional charge.

Although the cost varies, most are based on the affordability of those living on fixed income. Many are subsidized by HUD or various other city, county or state government programs. Contact the Area Agency on Aging for locations and more information.

Retirement Homes with Assisted Living Services

Today's Assisted Living Facilities (ALF) resemble large hotels that may house 60 to 300 older adults who reside in individual living units. Each private unit has a small kitchenette with a built-in hot plate, a small refrigerator, and a microwave oven plus the bathroom is equipped with safety bars and emergency pull cords. The monthly rental fee includes two-to-three meals per day, weekly housekeeping, scheduled transportation and a variety of planned activities. Although the cost varies, the majority are designed with moderate- to high-level income adults in mind and usually require a yearly contract.

Since older adults tend to wait until they have several chronic health problems before moving to an ALF, they usually need one or more of the assisted living services. The added services (ADLs) include medication management, assistance with bathing, dressing, and walking to the dining room. All of these services incur an additional cost.

Large assisted living facilities are not for those older adults who are suffering from any kind of progressive dementia.

Residential Care Facility (RCF) or Board and Care Home

This type of home is located in a residential neighborhood and is licensed to accommodate four to six older adults. These homes are ideal for individuals who require a protective environment with additional supervision for hygiene, medication, diet, and ambulation. Though ideal for those with dementia, not all RCFs accept those suffering from Alzheimer's disease or related dementias.

The better RCFs do not mix the dementia or confused individual with alert residents who are physically frail. Always inquire about the functional capabilities of residents and ask if the RCF is licensed for ambulatory and/or non-ambulatory residents. The cost varies with the location and amount of care required, such as incontinent care. Incontinent supplies are usually furnished for an extra cost. Some RCFs have given their caregivers training in dementia care and hospice care, which means these facilities have special waivers so they can care for residents as the disease progresses until the end of life.

Nursing or Convalescent Home

Often referred to as a Skilled Nursing Facility (SNF), these facilities are for those older adults who require rehabilitation from surgery, stroke, or other disabling illnesses. SNFs also offer custodial care when the patient is bed bound and no longer able to provide self-care, such as eating, turning over in bed, or requiring a feeding tube. Be aware that Medicare pays only for the rehabilitative services deemed necessary by a physician. **Medicare does not pay for custodial care.** MediCal or MediCaid, the state long-term care assistance programs, may share or cover the costs of this type of care, depending on the older adults finances. Ask if the SNF accepts MediCal or MediCaid.

Memory Care Units or Facilities

Due to the increasing numbers of older adults with dementia and memory loss, specialized facilities have been created for their care. These facilities can be units contained within a large assisted living facility or can be dedicated stand-alone buildings. The larger stand-alone facilities can house many individuals and sometimes these offer separate areas where residents stay according to their level of dementia, from early to moderate to late stage. The caregivers are trained in dementia care and residents can remain there until the end of the life. All aspects of care are covered for one price, however the cost is high which often comes as a surprise to families. The alternative is placing the loved one with dementia in a SNF, where they are usually sedated so they can be controlled and kept from wandering.

Life-Care or Continuing Care Community

This is a large planned residential community in a campus-like setting that offers all of the previous levels of care at one site: independent living, assisted living, RCF, and SNF. Some may have specialized dementia units. Depending on the ambiance of this type of option, a sizable entry or endowment fee is required which guarantees the older adult resident admission to all levels of care as may be required over the remaining course of life. An additional monthly fee covers meals, housekeeping, transportation and activities.

With each level of care the monthly fee goes up. Some Life Care Communities are contracted to care for the older adult even if they run out of money and are no longer able to pay. Of course, a thorough financial review is required before entry into a Life Care Facility, so that the chances of people running out of money are reduced for the contracting facility. The big advantage of this type of facility is the security and knowing that all levels of care are available at one location if the older adult requires it.

Which is the right choice?

Which is the most appropriate housing or living arrangement? Which ALF, RCF or SNF is better than others? Many factors are to be considered: the older adult's health, ability to manage living alone, cook, personal hygiene, finances, the location and condition of the present home. Most importantly, what kinds of assistance will the older adult need in the not- too-distant future.

Before considering any of the above-mentioned housing options, consider a consultation with a professional geriatric care manager and/or elder law attorney. They are extremely knowledgeable about the most appropriate resources and options, and the legal and financial resources that will be required to provide the most appropriate level of care.

Helping the older adult to realize, sooner rather than later, that they can make a new home in a safer and more suitable environment, if their physical and mental capacity diminishes, is well worth the effort. As with most changes involving an older adult's independence and control, it takes time, patience and tenacity.

What to look for when Considering an Alternative Living Arrangement

Is a new living arrangement affordable to the older adult? _____ *Yes* _____ *No*

Would a new living arrangement be affordable if you or other family members supplemented their income? _____ *Yes* _____ *No*

How much could these family members contribute per month? $ ________

Consider the following when selecting an alternative living arrangement:

- Visit at least three facilities that offer the appropriate level of care
- Talk to the residents and families of these facilities
- Examine and compare costs of care
- Plan/secure financial arrangements
- Plan to discuss/educate all family members on this decision

Evaluate each facility that you visit using the following guidelines:

Location — Is the facility close to the primary physician, hospital, family, and friends?

Activities — Does the facility have an activity program based on the residents needs and capabilities? (The number and diversity of activities depends on the abilities of the residents: exercise, bridge, day-trips, social events, music, or art therapy, etc.)

Buildings and Grounds — Is the facility well maintained, clean and attractive inside and out?

Safety and Security — Is the facility safe and secure? Depending on the type of facility, is there an emergency pull-cord in the bathroom and bedroom? How many entrances/exits does the facility have? How are these monitored (for example, security guards, alarms, or in-residence caregivers)?

Have you checked with the county ombudsman or community licensing office about any complaints that the facility may have incurred?

Living Quarters — Is there adequate personal space, privacy, and ventilation for each resident? Can the resident bring in personal furnishings and mementos? Are the common areas roomy and comfortable for the number of residents? Are the door jams wide enough for wheelchairs?

Financial Requirements — Is the monthly fee subject to a cost of living increase? Is a deposit required? What does the monthly fee cover, (for example, linens, personal laundry, outside activities, medication management, assistance with bathing and dressing, incontinent supplies)?

Meals — Are special meals available for conditions such as diabetes, low sodium diets or vegetarian needs? Can meals be brought to residents who are unable to eat in the area? Are nutritionally appropriate snacks readily available?

Medication — Does the facility have a strong medication management program? Does the staff monitor residents on new medication for possible side effects?

Staff — Does the staff pay attention to residents needs and desires? Do they treat each individual resident with respect? Depending on the facility and its level of care, what is the ratio of staff members to residents? Does the facility have frequent turnover of staff? Are you able to comfortably communicate with the staff of the facility? Are the administrators/manager of the facility accessible and approachable?

Family and Friends — Are family and friends able to visit or drop-in at any time? Can the resident be taken out for family events or community activities? Have you asked for references from other residents' families?

CHAPTER 11: CARING WOMAN TIPS
Decision Time: When is it?

There is no one definite answer to this question. Each primary caregiver and each family's level of tolerance varies however some of the turning points may be:

- If the physical care is beyond the primary caregiver's or family's ability to cope
- If pain management is difficult to control
- If the older adult no longer recognizes the primary caregiver or other close family members.
- If the physical and emotional strain of the older adult's care is jeopardizing the health and well-being of the primary caregiver.

- If the physical disabilities or dementia symptoms can no longer be managed at home.
- If the financial means of paying for in-home paid care providers is almost depleted

STEPS TO DECISION-MAKING:

1. Obtain a reliable health diagnosis and prognosis from the older adult's primary care physician.
2. Make a list of the pros and cons of each caregiving choice.
3. Locate and evaluate community resources that can provide the appropriate care to meet the needs of the older adult.
4. Call a family meeting and invite all family members, even the ones that may not want to be involved. If you are concerned about opposition, hire a geriatric care manager or social worker to mediate the meeting.
5. Discuss the present situation, making the older adult's needs the primary focus.
6. Set realistic goals.
7. Keep family members up-to-date regarding any changes in the level of care required whether or not they want to be involved.

8. Make decisions on a trial basis.

9. Always be prepared to revise the plans.

Chapter 12:

EVERYDAY HEROES AND THE REWARDS

"Kindness is the language which the deaf can hear and the blind can see." **— A quote from Mark Twain, a secular moralist**

Caregivers too often see themselves as taking on difficult responsibilities or doing a duty. I see them as ***everyday heroes***. These folks have many of the qualities that you expect to see in heroes: courage, stamina, perseverance, along with strength of body, mind and spirit. In addition, they often display attitudes of cheerfulness and hope that help to maintain energy for the valiant efforts required.

As a good daughter and caring woman, you have learned that attending to an older adult has uncommon challenges. There are times when you may only feel the weight of your responsibilities and you neglect to take credit for what you are giving your aging loved one. The many roles you take on as a caregiver and the resourcefulness needed to accomplish them makes you an *everyday hero*.

The life and death issues of a loved one who is chronically or terminally ill may never be far from your mind. What you do for them through your reassurance and kindness as they approach the end of their human journey takes strength of mind and spirit. Facing additional issues that may involve siblings, close relatives, past estrangements or long-buried family secrets takes courage. The physical efforts and mental fortitude require perseverance and stamina. This makes you an *everyday hero*.

The Rewards

The rewards that heroes receive are not always tangible ones and yet you have overcome challenging obstacles and gained a sense of accomplishment during this journey. Caregiving will test everything you have to give: patience, physical strength and emotional endurance in learning to balance family and personal responsibilities along with the care of an aging loved one. This journey can be extremely stressful and yet it does have its rewards and its blessings.

Caregiving teaches patience, compassion and resourcefulness. You learn patience when you help the older adult face declining memory or physical ability. You learn compassion when you observe their physical discomfort and emotional frustration that come with trying to do, and not being able to do, the things the inner spirit desires. When you find relatives and friends to help, community resources that offer support, and creative ways of performing routine chores, you learn resourcefulness.

The caregiving journey can also be a time of renewal for relationships among siblings, parents and grandchildren. It make take planning and courage to ask for help from other family members who can make your burden lighter, rekindling warmth and love that may have been missing in recent years. The realization that you are losing the patriarch or matriarch offers new appreciation of each moment, hour and day.

Being with someone who is near death can be a positive experience. I was holding my dad's hand as he breathed his last. He was in a coma the last three weeks and I had learned that even the unconscious can hear what we say to them. I told him I loved him, that he had done a fine job of being a husband, father and provider. These were his concerns, as he believed that he would meet his Maker and be judged after dying. Although I felt sad to lose his love and friendship, I felt it was a gift and blessing to be with him as he finished his journey.

Using Your Spiritual Gifts:

"The fruit of the Spirit is love, joy, peace, patience, kindness, goodness, faithfulness, gentleness and self-control" — Galatians 5:22.

Honoring an older adult by giving them the care they need at the end of life can be a spiritual experience. In your busy schedule of life and caregiving perhaps you may not have thought about the spiritual gifts you are using every minute of every day. We are as much spiritual beings as we are physical beings. The spirit, that inner part of us that relates to truth, beauty and goodness, is gaining attention as researchers have identified a positive spirit as being an important contributor to a longer, happier life. Developing our spiritual perspective enables us to find meaning at every stage of life and helps ease the fears and stress associated with the many changes that occur in our lives. This is especially true as you experience the caregiving journey and its final destination.

Spirituality is a rather elusive term and means different things to different people. While many associate it with religion, or belief in a Higher Power, others think of it as an inner feeling of serenity or peace. These are the feelings we associate with seeing a newborn baby, smelling a flower, taking a hike in the woods, sitting on a beach watching the waves. Your spirituality can be anything that brings you tranquility.

Along with physical exercise, we need spiritual exercise. Enhancing our spiritual self through spiritual exercises can help maintain a positive outlook, which is especially important as you experience the stress associated with caregiving.

Spiritual exercise need not be difficult or tedious; it just needs to become a routine part of daily life. Like physical exercise, spiritual exercises are matter of personal appeal and choice. Reading poetry, spiritual books, listening to comforting music may appeal to some. Meditation, contemplation or prayer may be suitable for others. Many also find spiritual refreshment in natural environments of seaside, mountains or desert. Just being quiet is also a spiritual activity.

Although some of these may not be appropriate for you now, you can find a quiet place to sit or rest for five or ten minutes. Take this brief time to contemplate your gifts, your talents and your accomplishments. Your everyday world may not be serene; however, for those few minutes you will be at peace. It may take practice, especially at first, but it is well worth it.

For years, we've heard that love makes the world go around; in reality it is the action of loving that makes the world a better place. The tedious moments in caregiving are part of the journey. It is our individual spiritual style that can make our personal world more promising, which benefits everyone. Spiritual exercise will bring calm, patience and acceptance to your inner spirit. These, in turn, create a state of well-being that makes this time of giving care more acceptable.

Be Good To You

Taking care of others requires taking care of you. Caregiving is physically difficult and can be an emotional seesaw. Acknowledge conflicting and confusing feelings. They are perfectly normal. Seek support from family, friends, a family caregiver, a support group and/or a faith community. Learn to take credit for the time and hard work you contribute to caregiving. A support group can be an excellent environment in which to talk about feelings of isolation, frustration or helplessness and to hear about the similar experiences of others. Your family may not want to listen, but these folks will.

Think of the future *before* the caregiving role ends. Getting lost in the role makes it hard to reclaim some semblance of normalcy after that role is over. Conflicting and confusing emotions can surround the loss of the older adult and of the caregiving role. You may be glad that your loved one is no longer suffering, but angry about having sacrificed so much—which may have included a job, friendships, hobbies and energy. There may be feelings of relief that the time of caregiving is finished - and guilty feelings about that relief.

The transition of returning to the before-caregiving life may not be easy. You will need to take steps during the journey so you do not lose sight of who you are. Making and taking time for friends, special interests and spiritual renewal is not an act of selfishness; it is one of self-preservation for the body, the mind and the spirit. Staying involved in things that are meaningful, even though time is limited, will help keep your life in balance and is the key to maintaining self-identity.

When the caregiving journey is over and the after-duties are accomplished, give yourself a reward. Plan a vacation, or take a "good daughter trip" like I did to visit some special friends in France. I had put off this trip for ten years while I was the caring daughter for my dad. It was a nice reward, along with knowing I had done my best, given the circumstances. Although I still was grieving his loss, I was ready to enjoy all that my friends and experiences had to offer.

Remember to give yourself a hug every day, a smile many times along the way and know that you are doing the best you can do, right here and right now. Caregivers are some of the loveliest and most generous people in the world and, I repeat, are truly **everyday heroes**.

GLOSSARY:

Health and Social Services Terms

Aging Life Care Association—(formerly National Association of Geriatric Care Managers) has listings of Geriatric Care Managers (GCM) nationwide who are specialists in helping families who are caring for older relatives. www.aginglifecare.org

Area Agency on Aging (AAA)—This office is responsible for planning effective use of "Federal Older Americans Act" funds which provide services to older Americans, generally defined as persons 60 years or older. The AAA undertakes studies regarding the needs of each county's senior citizens, develops plans to meet those needs for consideration by the county's Board of Supervisors, and then administers contracts to allocate Older American Act funds to nonprofit and government agencies that provide those services. A partial list of services includes hot meals in-home support services, peer counseling, senior center operation and a federally funded employment program for community service jobs for low income seniors. AAA can also be known as the County Office on Aging.

Acute Illness—A serious illness such as a heart attack or stroke that develops rapidly with pronounced symptoms.

The illness can also be of short duration such as influenza or pneumonia.

Activities of Daily Living (ADLS)—An individual's daily routine that allows him or her to maintain physical well-being, including: medication management, bathing, dressing, continence, eating, grooming, toileting and walking.

Adult Day Care Services—A multipurpose daytime program of recreation and social activities as well as hot meals for those living at home or in an assisted living facility. These can be provided at a community center, church or a specific location dedicated to that purpose. The care usually focuses on the physically and/or mentally impaired older adult, depending on the model: social daycare or health daycare. The social model offers supervised social and educational activities including exercise, music, art, memory games, guest speakers and family counseling. The health care model offers similar services to the social model with the addition of therapeutic health services such as nursing services, rehabilitation services of physical, occupational and speech therapies. Adult Day Care is designed not only for the elderly but also as a relief to family caregivers while at work or for those who need a break from the 24/7 care of an older adult with declining abilities. Attending an adult day center may delay or prevent the older adult from their admission to residential long-term care.

Assisted Living Facility (ALF)—A term used to describe large housing facilities that offer assistance in monitoring medications, bathing, dressing, and/or ambulation for older adults. The focus is on maintaining the individual's functioning and autonomy in her/his own apartment. Meals, social activities, weekly housekeeping and scheduled transportation are included in the monthly fee. The various assisted services cost extra and are based on the level of need.

Care Management—Assessing, arranging and overseeing an individual's living and healthcare routine by a trained professional. Contact the **Aging Life Association** (formerly NAPGCM) at www.aginglifecare.org for a referral near you or your elderly relative.

Caregiver Support Groups—A meeting lead by a professional or trained volunteer that provides a structured time for family caregivers to share their common concerns, express feelings, coping skills, learn about aging issues and resources and exchange information about their personal caregiving situation. The support group leader facilitates the discussion and provides educational and resource materials for participants. These groups can be found by calling a Senior Center, Alzheimer's Association or a local/regional hospital.

Chronic Illness—A physical or mental disability of an individual that continues or recurs frequently over a long period of time.

Continence/Incontinence—The ability or inability to voluntarily control urinary or fecal discharge.

Continuing Care Retirement Community (CCRC)—This housing option, sometimes called a Life Care Community, generally requires an individual to be able to live independently upon becoming a resident of the community. If and when the resident begins to need more assistance, specific additional services are made available. Most CCRCs offer three levels of housing: fully independent living, assisted living (personal care services), and skilled nursing care. Some may offer a Memory Care unit. A CCRC guarantees housing and care across the continuum in that one community so the resident does not have to move again.

Generally, a CCRC will charge an entrance fee as well as a monthly payment for its residential, personal care and nursing services. The entrance fee, formerly nonrefundable, now is generally refundable on departure under a variety of specified conditions.

Custodial Care—Help and supervision with activities of daily living: personal hygiene, dressing, eating, incontinence and similar functions in a residential or nursing home setting.

Dementia—A clinical term used to describe a group of brain disorders that disrupt and impair cognitive functions that are: thinking, memory, judgment, personality, mood and social functioning. These include Alzheimer's Disease, vascular dementia, Parkinson's Disease, Huntington's Disease and others mentioned in Chapter 7.

Discharge Planner or Case Manager—The professional staff member of a hospital or nursing home who develops a plan for the future care of a patient prior to discharge. This individual may provide references to resources that offer home health care, residential care or other related options.

Do Not Resuscitate (DNR) Order—A legal document signed by the care recipient, physician, and primary (family) caregiver that expresses the older adult's desire not to be given CPR or any resuscitative/reviving measures to bring back life. Since a call to 911 summons the paramedics, the care recipient will automatically be revived. If a DNR is in place, call the emergency room of the local hospital instead of 911.

Durable Power of Attorney for Health Care (DPAHC)—The DPAHC is a legally binding document that allows you to choose someone to express your health care wishes if you are unable to do so. With a DPAHC, you maintain control over your health care. If you are incapacitated, your agent may: a) consent to treatment, b) refuse treatment, c) with draw consent for treatment.

Elderlaw Attorney—An attorney specializing in improving the availability and delivery of legal services to older adults and belongs to the National Academy of Elderlaw Attorneys (NAELA). Contact: www.naela.org

Geriatric Assessment Program—A complete evaluation of an older adult's physical, psychological, an social conditions by a professional team of specialists. This team makes recommendations to the older adult, family members and primary care physician. Because the health problems of older individuals are frequently complex and interrelated to their social and emotional lives, this team approach to diagnosis and treatment offers a method of untangling what often proves to be interconnected health problems. This type of evaluation is highly recommended for those suffering from symptoms of dementia. These programs are usually found at universities with medical schools or teaching hospitals.

Geriatric Care Manager (GCM)—A certified professional specializing in assisting older adults and their families with the decisions and resources relating to long-term care arrangements. A GCM has extensive knowledge about the cost, quality, and availability of resources and services in the community. They offer consultations and assessments to identify needs, and offer guidance in the selection of services appropriate to the older adult's needs. Refer to Aging Life Care Association for referrals.

Geriatrician—A medical doctor with special education and training in the diagnosis and treatment of older adults. Geriatricians offer a more holistic approach to their evaluation of the older adult's health challenges.

Geriatric Social Worker—A licensed professional who assists older adults and their families to understand and cope with the social, emotional, and psychological aspects of aging. The social worker acts as coordinator, director and teacher in assessing services.

Gerontologist—An individual who, in addition to having an existing degree in nursing, social work, psychology, or social services, has received advanced training in the biological, psychological, and sociological aspects of aging.

Healthcare Proxy—A healthcare proxy has the same effect as a durable medical power of attorney with one difference: a lawyer is not usually required to complete the sample preprinted form.

Health Insurance Counseling Advocacy Program (HICAP)—Advocacy for Medicare related questions. Offers help by giving information on supplemental insurance and long-term care insurance purchasing, billing and claims filing. Comparison sheets of LTC Insurance and supplemental are available to the consumer before purchase. This is a free service. Most states have this program; however not all are called by this title. Call your nearest AAA for specific name, website and phone number.

Health Maintenance Organizations (HMOs)—A health plan that combines coverage of health-care costs and delivery of health care for a prepaid premium. Medicare pays the premium for those over 65 who sign up and become members with a specific HMO provider. Members receive services from personnel employed by or under contract to the HMO. HMOs generally require members/patients to select a primary care physician (PCP) who will coordinate the patient's care. The member usually needs a referral from the PCP before he/she can go to a specialist or a hospital. Call the HICAP office near you for a comparison sheet of HMOs serving your area.

Hospice—A special way of caring for terminally ill adults and children. Hospice exists to provide support and care for individuals in the last phases of life so they might live as fully and comfortably as possible. Utilizing the expertise of Hospice in connection with the patient's physician can eliminate much of the pain/anxiety. Hospice recognizes dying as a normal process and neither hastens or postpones death. Medicare/HMOs cover part of the costs involved in Hospice care.

Housing Options—Also referred to as Alternative Living Arrangements and include Senior Apartments, Assisted Living Facilities (ALF), Residential Care Facilities (RCF), Skilled Nursing Facilities (SNF), Life Care or Continuing Care Retirement Communities (CCRC). Refer to Chapter 11 for descriptions.

In-Home Health Care—Qualified nurses or aides that come to the home to provide medical or personal-care services. There are several classifications: Registered or Licensed Vocational Nurse, Certified Nurse's Aide or Home Health Aide. All have special training in various levels of care and can be hired on for a short shift, long shift or live-in basis. Qualifications are extremely important as is a compatible personality.

Instrumental Activities of Daily Living (IADLs)—Those household activities that allow an individual to maintain basic living needs: meal preparation, shopping, transportation and laundry.

Long-Term Care(LTC)—A range of medical, nursing, custodial, social and community services designed to help individuals maintain as much independence as possible within the limits of their abilities. The need for assistance usually results from a chronic or disabling mental or physical condition.

Long-Term Care Insurance (LTC)—Insurance policies issued by private companies to assist with the costs of long-term care in nursing facilities, residential care or in-home care. Most policies begin to pay when the beneficiary requires assistance with 2 or more ADLs. The amount and terms of coverage vary with the purchase price. Call HICAP for a comparison sheet of LTC policies.

LTC Ombudsman Program—Provides advocacy for older adult residents of long-term care facilities including: skilled nursing, residential care and assisted living facilities. Services of this program offer information on choosing a care facility, education on resident's rights and facility regulations, assistance with Advanced Health Directives, complaint investigation and resolution, plus consultations and referrals. Services are free and confidential.

Medicare—The federal health-insurance program that helps defray many of the medical expenses of most Americans over the age of 65. Individuals eligible for Social Security may apply for Medicare benefits. Older individuals should apply for Medicare benefits three months prior to their 65th birthday. For information about how to apply for Medicare, contact your local Social Security office. Working individuals over the age of 65 are entitled to Medicare even though they do not apply for Social Security.

Medicare has four parts:

PART A: This is hospital insurance that helps pay the cost of inpatient hospital care. In some instances and under certain conditions, Part A helps pay for inpatient care in a skilled-nursing facility, for home-health care and for hospice care. Older individuals and their families need to be knowledgeable about Medicare coverage as it has some limitations for out-of-hospital care. Detailed information about Medicare benefits and explanation of coverage can be obtained by calling the local Social Security office.

PART B: This is medical insurance that helps pay for medically necessary doctor's services, outpatient hospital services and some other medical services. Medicare enrollees must pay a monthly premium for Part B. Contact the local Social Security office for more information.

Part C: Known as **Medicare Advantage (MA)**, this is an alternative to the Original Medicare fee-for-service and Medicare beneficiaries have the option to enroll in a MA plan. Medicare pays private insurance companies to provide health services to beneficiaries who have enrolled in these plans. Joining one of these plans is optional. To join an MA plan, one must be enrolled in both Medicare Part A *and* Part B and continue to pay the Part B premium. An individual receives Medicare-covered benefits through the plan and retain the full rights and protections entitled to all Medicare beneficiaries. Enrollment in one of these plans is based on a calendar year and an individual has the option of changing MA plans or returning to Original Medicare, each year during the Annual Election Period. Before signing an application for an MA plan, be sure to understand ***all*** of the terms and conditions.

PART D: Prescription Drug Coverage. Prescription coverage is authorized under Medicare Part D. These plans are sold by contracted private insurance companies who must follow Medicare standards. Enrollment is optional however there is penalty for late enrollment. To enroll in a Part D plan, an individual must have either Medicare Part A or B. These plans vary in monthly premiums, deductibles and copayments and most importantly, the list of drugs included in the plan, referred to as the formulary. These plans and the formularies change every year, so it is important to review them every year and, if desired, change the plan during the Annual Election Period. The Medicare office www.medicare.gov or HICAP offers assistance in choosing a plan.

Medicaid (known as Medi-Cal in California)—A health care program for low-income individuals cooperatively financed by federal and state governments and administered by the states to those who are eligible. Benefits cover outpatient and some institutional care. The coverage for the different levels of institutional care varies from state to state. Each state has a set of criteria that establishes eligibility for services under its specific program. Further information about the Medicaid (Medi-Cal) program is available at the local county health and social service departments or the AAA Senior Information and Referral Office.

Medicare Supplemental Insurance—May also be referred to as Medigap. These are commercially sold insurance policies tailored to provide supplemental coverage for individuals on Medicare. Depending on the policy, Medigap policies pay some or all of Medicare deductibles and copayments. Coverage varies with the type of policy purchased and pays only up to the amount covered by Medicare.

Palliative Care—Treats and manages symptoms rather than the disease. The focus on palliative care is assisting the individual in living well as they can today. This type of care is offered under three circumstances: *Acute Palliative care* manages the symptoms after an illness, injury or surgery. This is short term care. *Chronic Palliative care* manages symptoms related to ongoing, serious or illness such as congestive heart disease, kidney or liver disease or ALS. *End-of-Life Palliative care* manages symptoms when curative treatments are not working and based on the best of medical knowledge that the individual has a limited time to live. Here comfort and quality of life becomes the focus. It is important to note that with end-of-life palliative care a patient can receive care to prevent and relieve suffering during their life-limiting illness while still receiving treatments such as chemo, radiation, surgery, intravenous therapy and dialysis. Palliative care allows patients to continue to pursue "curative" medical treatments while receiving symptom management. To be eligible for in-home palliative care paid by Medicare and other insurances the patient must be "homebound" and a doctor must certify that.

National Academy Of Elder Law Attorneys—Member attorneys of this organization are dedicated to improving the quality of legal services provided to people as they age and people with special needs. www.naela.org

Patient Bill of Rights—A list of policies and procedures to be followed to ensure that individuals receiving healthcare service will be treated with dignity and can participate fully in decisions relevant to their healthcare.

Personal Emergency Response System—Equipment that monitors the safety of older adults while living at home. The older adult usually wears an activator that she/he can push or squeeze when an emergency arises. The activator sends a signal to a response station, which in turn, triggers an immediate call to the older adult or a predetermined relative, neighbor or friend. The cost of these systems varies and is usually paid for by the older adult or the family.

Primary Care Physician—The doctor who is consulted first when a health problem occurs and on whom the patient relies for on-going care, advice and referrals. With HMOs the primary care physician must authorize all referrals to other doctors.

Primary Caregiver—The individual who has the main responsibility for taking care of another person and is usually the one who organizes the care and services the older adult needs. Each and every family has one member who is or will become the primary caregiver. This individual takes on the responsibility for making the health, caregiving and organizational decisions on behalf of the older adult, however this individual is not always the hands-on caregiver.

Respite Care—Long-term care services provided to the older adult on a temporary basis to give a much needed break to the primary caregiver. Assisted living and residential care facilities may offer such service proved they have a vacancy. Adult Day Care is another resource that can be utilized for respite.

Senior Citizens Information and Referral (SCIR)—Provides access to agencies and programs set up to help older adults. Senior Information and Referral maintains a file of governmental and private non-profit human service programs. Services of this agency not only include I & R but also follow up and community education to groups serving older adults. Older adults and others are encouraged to call to learn which service programs are available to help solve a problem pertaining to a particular need.

Senior Centers—Serve as focal points of information and services for older adults. Senior centers are owned and operated by separate and various organizations such as cities and/or non-profit organizations. Each senior center has a unique array of services and means to respond to the need of the community. Services available may include: senior lunch services, information, community education, recreation activities, socialization, music, health screenings, arts and crafts, and health insurance counseling. Some senior centers offer computer classes and have computers available for use and others make loans of medical equipment.

Shared Housing—This type of program matches older citizens with other older adults or younger individuals. The benefits of shared housing include reduced living costs, improved standard of living, shared household responsibilities, companionship and help in emergencies. Be very clear with possible applicants about what lifestyles and behaviors are acceptable and not acceptable. These programs can be located by calling your local Area Agency on Aging.

United States Department of Veteran Affairs—Recognizes veterans special circumstances and provides assistance to qualifying veterans to pay for health benefit programs, such as adult day care, in-home care, or assisted living. To qualify, the veteran must have been in active service, received an honorable discharge and have served a continuous 24 months (only for those enlisted after 1980.) Call your local VA office to enroll which can be found at www.va.gov.

Notes: